INFERTILITY

The Essential Guide

Jane
Dean

Infertility – The Essential Guide is also available in accessible formats for people with any degree of sight loss. The large print edition and ebook (with accessibility features enabled) are available from Need2Know. Please let us know if there are any special features you require and we will do our best to accommodate your needs.

First published in Great Britain in 2011 by
Need2Know
Remus House
Coltsfoot Drive
Peterborough
PE2 9JX
Telephone 01733 898103
Fax 01733 313524
www.need2knowbooks.co.uk

Contents

Chapter Two

Exploring Natural Fertility

Very few of us actually observe the workings of our own body until something goes wrong. However, when planning your baby's conception, it pays to become very aware of how your body is functioning. For women this will give you an indication of your most fertile time and for men a feeling of being healthy and in control.

So where do we start? The most obvious is the menstrual period and charting the changes, both physical and mental, which occur during a complete cycle.

The menstrual cycle is orchestrated by the presence of hormones in the blood. The conductor is the hypothalamus, a portion of the brain which controls hormone output. The average monthly cycle for women is 28 days, but this can vary and for some women 33 days may be normal. Confusingly, a cycle can change from month to month and it is important at this stage to understand that our emotions also have an influence upon hormone balance. The hypothalamus is also controlling the release of stress hormones which can have a negative influence upon the monthly cycle.

In medical terms, the first day of your period is termed Day 1, when a hormone called gonadotropin-releasing (GnRH), tells the pituitary to release yet another hormone, FSH. Slowly over the next two weeks, FSH instructs the follicles within the ovaries to start growing. As these immature eggs start to grow they produce oestrogen, which in turn stops the production of FSH and prepares an egg for ovulation. The pituitary gland then releases yet another hormone, luteinising hormone (LH) which stimulates ovulation.

This chemical messaging service occurs every month without our full awareness, however we can observe certain signs which indicate how this activity is progressing.

'When planning your baby's conception, it pays to become very aware of how your body is functioning.'

One of those signs is vaginal mucus. When ovulation is about to take place, a particular type of mucus is produced from the cervix and appears at the vagina. This can be the first sign of the approaching fertile phase of the monthly cycle. At this time, the vaginal mucus becomes more watery. This watery, egg white-type mucus is essential to sperm survival; not only does it allow better mobility to the swimming sperm, but it provides essential nutrients to help them survive. Healthy sperm can live for five to six days in mucus that is hospitable.

It takes several hours for the sperm to swim through the cervix and uterus and on to the fallopian tubes. If the vaginal environment is hostile, particularly too acidic, then the sperm will rapidly become immobilised (see chapter 4), fertile mucus should be slightly alkaline.

The cycle

Based on a cycle that starts with Day 1 as the first day of your period, the first 5 days are the menstrual flow.

- Days 6 and 7 are dry days.
- Days 8, 9 and 10 the mucus is whitish, sticky and tacky.
- Days 11 and 12 the mucus is thinner and becoming slippery.
- Days 13 and 14 the mucus is clear, slippery and stretchy, egg white-type mucus.
- Days 15 and 16 the mucus is less slippery and more creamy.
- Days 17 to 28 dry or sticky mucus in a random pattern.

The changes in the mucus are mainly under the control of hormones but a nutritious diet can improve it further. Any vaginal infection will alter the mucus pattern and will be impossible to monitor until the infection has been treated and cleared.

Remember fertile mucus is:

- Clear, a bit like raw egg white.
- Thin and watery, it can feel very wet and dries leaving no residue.

- Slippery and lubricating.
- Stretchy and holds the stretch.

Other possible fertile signs:

- At the point of ovulation, the hormone progesterone is released causing a slight rise in temperature.
- There may be some slight abdominal discomfort.
- Some women experience a slight bleed or 'spotting' (medical term 'mittelschmerz').
- Breast tenderness, a tingling sensation due to the effect of oestrogen.
- An increased sexual urge, always a good thing when baby-making.

If you are planning a pregnancy, it makes sense to have intercourse when you ovulate, so days 13 and 14, when the mucus is most favourable, and you have a heightened sexual desire. Sexual energy or libido, plays an important role as female orgasm is more easily achieved during this phase. The rhythmic contractions of vagina and penis simultaneously aide the swimming sperm forward and upwards on their long journey towards the fallopian tubes. Although it is very pleasurable to share orgasm together, it is not necessary for fertilisation to take place. It is more important that both partners are relaxed with each other's company and enjoy the sexual experience.

The lifespan of an egg is only estimated to be between eight and 12 hours, although some publications argue that the egg can survive up to 24 hours. It remains a very small window of opportunity and the healthier you are, the more likely it is that your egg will last longer. Sperm, on the other hand can survive inside your body for up to one week. This is for a very good reason. It is seldom possible, during sexual activity to determine the exact point of ovulation, so nature has made sure that sperm reaching the fallopian tubes, can survive for between three to six days while they are waiting for the appearance of an egg. So you can understand that even if you miss having sex at the time of ovulation, there is still a chance to conceive if sperms are already in situ.

'If you are planning a pregnancy, it makes sense to have intercourse when you ovulate, so days 13 and 14, when the mucus is most favourable, and you have a heightened sexual desire.'

The cervix

The cervix is the small, round, tight piece of muscle guarding the entrance to the uterus. The cervix remains tightly closed during the non-fertile period and is plugged with thick mucus. This acts as a deterrent to any invading microorganisms and is very necessary to keep our pelvic organs infection free. A tightly closed cervix also acts as a barrier to swimming sperm. However, when the fertile period approaches and the vaginal mucus becomes more slippery, the cervical opening is also relaxed and more oval-shaped.

The cervix can be felt manually. With washed hands, insert your index finger high into the vagina and feel for the round protrusion which is your cervix. This procedure is similar to inserting a tampon and once you have located your cervix within a very short space of time you will be able to recognise the difference between a non-fertile cervix and a more welcoming cervix. There is also a slight lowering of the position of the cervix during the fertile period.

A number of publications use examination of the cervix as an important marker of fertility, but, in my view, trying to find your cervix can be stressful and not necessarily an essential procedure. In my opinion, it is more important to become familiar with the changing pattern of the cervical mucus.

'Most couples chart the temperature for two or three months alongside observation of the mucus.'

Body temperature

We have already mentioned that the temperature rises slightly on ovulation due to an increase in progesterone. The rise in temperature is quite small, between 0.2° and 0.6° centigrade. Many women spend months charting their temperature until the activity becomes monotonous. For some women this is very reassuring to know they are ovulating, but the temperature of your body can change if you have been drinking alcohol, in hot weather or indeed if you are stressed. So again, although a helpful marker, not something you have to do every month. Most couples chart the temperature for two or three months alongside observation of the mucus.

Charts to record temperature, mucus and state of your cervix canbe downloaded free from the Fertility Education Trust (see help list).

Ovulation predictor kits

Ovulation predictor kits can be purchased from any good chemist. They measure the amount of LH, the hormone which stimulates ovulation.

Although these kits provide an extra marker for ovulation there is no evidence to suggest that using them will improve your chances of success. However, they can be used in conjunction with charting your cycle until you become so familiar with your own body that you will actually know when you are about to ovulate. These kits are more useful when you have a very irregular cycle.

There are two types of kit:

▓ Urine based – these require dipping a small predictor stick into a cup of urine. As the LH surge often begins during the night, an early morning test may not give the best result as the LH does not appear in the urine until several hours later. Manufacturers usually recommend testing between 10am and 8pm. Try to test at around the same time each day.

▓ Saliva based – this test is looking for a rise in oestrogen produced by the ripening egg. As oestrogen rises, the salt content in your saliva also increases. When the saliva dries, it forms a crystallised fern-like pattern which indicates a rise in salt. The test is simple, the kit arrives with a small pocket-sized microscope and a number of slides. Do not use too much saliva, either lick the slide or rub over saliva with a clean finger; wait until the slide is dry and then observe via the microscope.

Charting your cycle with observation of the cervical mucus is important to predict when the woman is at her most fertile. The chart shown overleaf can be downloaded from the Fertility Education Trust free of charge (see help list).

Semen strength

There is much controversy over this subject. It used to be believed that men had to conserve their semen when planning a baby. Men were told to avoid ejaculation for a time either from intercourse or masturbation to conserve numbers of sperm. This really is an old wives' tale and one which must be dismissed.

It is important to keep the sperm moving. Sperm are being produced all the time and although it is true, without an ejaculation, they will greatly increase in number but many of them will have been suffocated in the build-up and many more damaged to the point where they have little or no energy to swim. Remember, sperm can survive between three and six days in the fallopian tube, so restricting intercourse may also lessen the availability of waiting sperm.

Fertility Chart

Day of cycle		1	2	3	4	5	6	7	8	9	10	11	12	13	14	15	16	17	18	19	20	21	22	23	24	25	26	27	28	29	30	31	32
Period		X	X	X	X	X																								X			
Spotting							X																										
Sensation	Dry						X	X	X								X	X			X	X	X	X	X	X	X						
Colour	No mucus seen						X	X	X	X							X	X			X	X	X	X	X	X	X						
Sensation	Moist/damp									X	X	X				X			X	X								X	X				
Colour	White										X	X				X			X	X								X	X				
	Cloudy/opaque																																
Type	Milky/creamy										X	X																X	X				
	Clotty, crumbly, pasty																																
	Tacky, gluey, elastic															X			X	X													
Sensation	Wet												X	X	X																		
Colour	Cloudy/clear												X																				
	Clear, transparent													X	X																		
Type	Slippy, slimy, stretchy												X	X	X																		
	Like raw-egg													X	X	1	2	3	Infertile from night of PEAK + 3 / 3rd high temperature														
PEAK DAY		1	2	3	4	5	6	7	8	9	10	11	12	13	14	15	16	17	18	19	20	21	22	23	24	25	26	27	28	29	30	31	32

This chart is to record vaginal mucus. It can be used in conjunction with a temperature record chart also available from the Fertility Education Trust (see help list).

Summing Up

- Get to know your cycle by taking note of the subtle changes that happen when the body is preparing to ovulate. You can do this by monitoring changes in your mucus, examining your cervix, monitoring body temperature or using an ovulation predictor kit – using a combination of these might be the most reliable way.

- Keep a chart monitoring your mucus for a few months to help you understand your body's natural rhythm.

- If your cycle is irregular then an ovulation predictor kit may be useful.

- Do not restrict intercourse, allowing too much of a build-up of sperm could be damaging, sperm can survive for three to six days in the fallopian tube anyway, so there is no harm in having intercourse even if it's not the optimum time for ovulation.

Chapter Three

Fertility and Diet

Health of both partners

Creating new life is one thing, creating a healthy, vibrant, intelligent baby, free from congenital abnormality (birth defects) and birth injury is the goal we all seek to achieve. This is within our grasp and this is what nature intended. 'Choose your parents well', was a term often quoted by a special care baby paediatrician during my days as a midwife. What he was actually saying was, healthy parents produce healthy babies, which is simple common sense when you think about it.

Where do we start?

Start with the food we eat. The term 'diet' is bandied about so much it has become part of our everyday vocabulary as the government attempts to encourage us all to eat a healthy diet. However, improving your diet is one area where you alone are in control. No one is picking up the spoon and feeding you, you alone are in command. So, in theory this should be an easy challenge, but in my experience it can be difficult to accomplish successfully in the early days. To change the way we eat presents a number of problems. So let us look at the difficulties:

- We eat the foods we like and in turn they give us a feeling of satisfaction.

- We often eat similar foods and at similar times as our parents did.

- We believe our food is manufactured or farmed according to the highest standards.

- We believe that five-a-day, i.e. eating five fruits and vegetables a day, is what we need to do to stay healthy.
- We believe that low-fat diets are the answer to most health problems.

The difficulty in baby-making is often a direct result of a poor diet. We are not a starving population, in fact some nutrition specialists say we are 'overfed but undernourished'. Most of us eat at least one meal a day which we believe to be healthy. The problem lies with the lack of vitamins and minerals in the food we eat and our ability to absorb those essential nutrients.

You must think about what you are eating and drinking. If you can, try to eat organic foods whenever possible; they have been grown in soil which has not been subjected to a number of chemicals and have not been sprayed by harmful pesticides. Fruits and vegetables grown in this way have been shown to have a higher concentration of essential minerals and they also taste so much better.

Recent research from the Health Supplements Information Service (HSIS) found that women of childbearing age had a poor intake of key nutrients. One in five, 20%, of women failed to meet the basic intake levels for iron, 11% had low intakes of vitamin B2, while 9% did not get sufficient magnesium. Omega 3 fatty acids, found in fish oils, which are essential to foetal development, were less than half the recommended level.

HSIS also reviewed a number of scientific papers and found that pregnant women had inadequate intakes of iron, calcium, vitamin D, vitamin B12, magnesium and zinc compared to those who were not pregnant.

Good nutrition is essential for baby-making, both to reduce the risk of miscarriage and to give your baby the best possible chance of a healthy life. A good diet comprises of carbohydrates, fats, proteins and clean water. Within these food groups are all the essential vitamins and minerals required for baby-making.

By increasing your intake of essential vitamins and minerals, you will be providing a 'deposit account' for your baby, reserves that he or she can call upon during their early years and be thankful for in adulthood.

Vitamins and minerals

Vitamin or mineral...	Required for...	Found in...
Vitamin A	Eye health. Production of male and female sex hormones. Neurological and immune function.	Orange, yellow and red fruits and vegetables. Green leafy vegetables. Whole milk. Butter. Cheese. Oily fish. Eggs.
Vitamin B1 (thiamin)	Ovulation. Digestion. Nerve health.	Nuts. Wholegrain cereals. Also added to commercial cereals, pork and potatoes.
Vitamin B2 (riboflavin)	Immune health. Detoxification of oestrogens and progesterone.	Fish. Meat. Eggs. Cheese. Avocados. Mushrooms. Wholegrains.
Vitamin B3 (niacin)	Skin health. Nervous system health Digestion.	White meat. Beef. Fish. Nuts. Eggs. Milk. Cheese.
Vitamin B5 (pantothenic acid)	Fertility and hormone production. Foetal development.	Dried fruits. Dates. Prunes. Apricots. Red and white meat. Nuts. Chickpeas. Lentils.

Vitamin B6 (pyridoxine)	Essential for female hormone production. Immune health.	Brown rice. Yeast. Bananas. Red and white meat. Fish.
Vitamin B9 (folic acid)	Foetal development. Genetic health. Sperm development. Making red blood cells.	Green leafy vegetables Oranges. Beans. Nuts. Wholemeal bread. Fortified commercial breakfast cereals.
Vitamin B12 (cobalamin)	Genetic health. Sperm production. Anaemia prevention.	Red and white meat. Fish. Eggs. Commercial breakfast cereals.
Vitamin C (ascorbic acid)	Cell health. Antioxidant. Sperm health and motility. Fertility in men and women.	Oranges and orange juice. Green leafy vegetables, including broccoli. Blackcurrants. Red peppers. Potatoes.
Vitamin D	Healthy bones and teeth. Absorption of calcium and phosphorus.	Sunlight. Oily fish. Eggs.
Vitamin E (tocopherol)	Fertility in both men and women. Blood health. Powerful antioxidant.	Vegetable oils. Wheatgerm. Nuts. Seeds. Eggs. Broccoli.
Magnesium	Muscle and nerve health. Formation of bones and teeth. Necessary for calcium absorption. Maintenance of a healthy reproductive system.	Wholegrains. Green leafy vegetables. Nuts. Seeds.

Manganese	Essential for reproductive health, including ovulation. Healthy skin. Regulating blood sugar.	Wholegrains. Nuts. Seeds. Pineapple. Lentils.
Selenium*	Essential for reproductive health, particularly for sperm motility and prevention of cell damage.	Eggs. Meat. Fish. Brazil nuts. Wholegrains. Brown rice.
Zinc	Fertility. Essential for sperm health. Essential for egg production.	Nuts. Seeds. Eggs. Sweetcorn. Carrots. Wholegrains.
Iron	Red cell formation. Immune health. Prevention of anaemia. Prevention of miscarriage.	Green leafy vegetables. Liver. Red meat and game. Oily fish. Nuts. Figs. Wholegrains.
Essential fatty acids**	Healthy reproductive system.	Oily fish. Sunflower seeds. Olives. Linseeds.

* Selenium deficiency is not uncommon as intensive arable farming leaches selenium from the soil. Always include selenium in any nutritional supplementation.

** These fats are called essential because they must be obtained from the diet as the body does not make or store them in large quantities.

Carbohydrates

Complex carbohydrates from wholegrains are important, that is nothing added and nothing taken away, as we find in refined flour. Good sources are organic wholemeal breads, oatmeal, brown rice and some fresh fruits and vegetables. Always take the organic option when you can and always remember to wash fruits and vegetables before eating. This is particularly important if you have been unable to purchase organic products. Add a tablespoon of vinegar to the washing water to assist removal of pesticide residues.

Avoid simple carbohydrates found in white flour, white rice and pasta, and all refined sugars.

'Complex carbohydrates from wholegrains are important, that is nothing added and nothing taken away, as we find in refined flour.'

Proteins

Proteins are essential to the cells of enzymes, hormones, muscles and indeed all internal organs. Proteins are composed of various amino acids which are broken down during digestion to form other amino acids. A healthy digestive system is important.

Amino acids, which are the building blocks of protein, are essential to fertility. There are 20 amino acids identified in protein, eight of these are called 'essential' as they have to be found from the food we eat, the remaining 12, our bodies can produce providing we are adequately nourished. There are two amino acids, spermadine and aspermine, essential to sperm production and health, it is these two amino acids which give semen its characteristic odour.

Animal products and fish contain all the amino acids required for health. It is possible to obtain these from vegetarian sources by combining nuts, seeds and pulses together, although there is a greater availability from animal products.

Avoid non-organic meat and fish whenever possible. Avoid all processed meats including burgers, sausages, pies, salamis and pâtés.

Fats

Fats form an essential part of a healthy diet. Do not be afraid of eating fat. Organic bacon, all organic meats, organic butter and cream can be eaten in moderation without concern. Fats are vital to baby-making. All our cells require fats to function and these include all the special cells that make hormones, and hormone balance is so important to conception. Fats are required to help us absorb the fat-soluble vitamins, A, D, E and K.

Low-fat diets are not always the healthy option, although we have been persuaded that eating fat makes us fat, and being fat causes diabetes, infertility, heart disease and cancer. Clever marketing strategies have led us into believing polyunsaturated vegetable oils and margarines are the healthy option. However, butter fills the requirement for fat much more readily than a supposedly healthy polyunsaturated margarine.

Water

Water from the tap can be high in nitrates, be contaminated by lead, aluminium and more concerning, by oestrogen mimickers. These are commercially made chemicals which do not biodegrade and are harmful to both sexes. Exposure to synthetic oestrogen can cause enormous disruption to reproductive health. There are also residues of medical drugs found in water supplies, including antibiotics.

As water is required for hormone health you could get around this by installing a water filter at home or investing in a filter jug. Try to drink water only from glass bottles, as the plastic bottles can produce oestrogen mimickers which are particularly harmful to sperm production.

Try to drink at least two litres of water a day. This may seem an impossible task to some, but drink as much water as you are able and the remaining can be taken from diluted fruit juices or herb and fruit teas.

'Fats form an essential part of a healthy diet. Do not be afraid of eating fat.'

The perfect fertility diet?

It is difficult to be prescriptive on the perfect diet, as we are all individuals who have been formed from generations of mixed gene pools. For example, Western cultures may be able to digest dairy products much more easily than Eastern cultures, so designing the perfect diet must be tailored to the individual. However, there are certain guidelines which we can all follow and understand.

Taking into account the knowledge we now have of the various food groupings and the importance of organically-produced food, we can factor in the desirable amount of each food. The body functions best in a slightly alkaline environment. As all our cells require water, keeping the body pH slightly alkaline is dependent upon the foods we eat. The following list can act as a guideline when preparing meals. If the food on your plate consists of approximately 80% alkaline and 20% acid foods then you are giving your body the best chance to keep healthy. There is no need to weigh, just look at the food on your plate and make the estimate yourself.

- Acid-forming foods (20% of the food on your plate) – meat, fish, most cereals, eggs, cheese, nuts, prunes, plums, cranberries, whisky and beer.

- Alkaline-forming foods (80% of the food on your plate) – most fruits and vegetables, soya products, molasses and wine.

- Neutral foods – animal fats and oils.

- Anti-nutrients – those foods which add nothing by way of nutrition but use essential vitamins and minerals stored in the body during their elimination. These include, refined sugar, alcohol, tannins in tea and phytates (toxins found in plants) found in wheat and soya.

The 80-20 rule has long been part of naturopathic philosophy, but, as mentioned, individual dietary needs vary taking into account vegetarian requirements and those of meat-eating individuals. The best advice is to source foods that are organic, and grown and eaten as near to source as possible, and you should enjoy the food on your plate.

Checking your nutritional status

There are various ways of checking your nutritional status but the simplest and most effective is by hair mineral analysis (see help list). It can be harmful to take large doses of supplements without professional guidance as some supplements may adversely affect body chemistry. However, in the following list are supplements for fertility recommended by Marilyn Glenville PhD who has a professional interest in nutrition:

Nutrient	Female partner (mcg – microgram, mg – milligram)	Male partner (mcg – microgram, mg – milligram)
Folic acid	400mcg	-
Zinc	30mg	30mg
Selenium	100mcg	100mcg
Linseed oil	1,000mg	1,000mg
Vitamin B6	Up to 50mg	Up to 50mg
Vitamin B12	Up to 50mcg	Up to 50mcg
Vitamin E	300-400iu	300-400iu
Vitamin C	1,000mg	1,000mg
Manganese	5mg	5mg
L-arginine	-	300mg
L-carnitine	-	100mg

The diet of our parents and grandparents

As mentioned in the first chapter, a woman arrives at birth with her composite 400,000 eggs. Women who were born before or just after the second world war, consumed very little in the way of pesticides, hydrogenated, polyunsaturated fats, food colourings and harmful by-products of radioactive waste or indeed anything that we now know cause genetic disturbances or increase the risks of cancer and heart disease.

In recent years food production has improved, but for many years during the late 1950s, 1960s and early 1970s people were exposed to a whole array of unregulated and untested chemicals which would have been unwittingly consumed. The food which your mother or grandmother was eating may have upset the normal processes of cell production and repair. Nature being powerful, will fight back and any egg or sperm not in perfect health is liable to be rejected. This can result in an inability to conceive, an inability to hold on to a pregnancy with repeated miscarriages or sadly the birth of a baby with complex health problems, including developmental delay.

Do not despair with this rather gloomy picture, as you are now in the driving seat and understand the importance of good nutrition for maximum fertility. Research has shown that by taking adequate steps to improve nutritional status, fertility level is increased and successful pregnancies with healthy babies is a direct result. That is, ensuring a healthy diet will ensure a healthy pregnancy.

At this point, I can sense your impatience. Wanting a baby is all-consuming and you may feel that time is of the essence. Preparation can take up to a year and sometimes longer if nutritional status has been severely impaired. The results will be worth the wait. Improving one's own health before conception is the best and finest gift you can give your unborn child. Remember the quote, 'choose your parents well'. Should ART still be required, your chances of success on the first attempt will be improved dramatically if you have first improved your diet and nutrition.

Summing Up

- Think about what you eat and try to ensure you get the vitamins and minerals that your body needs. If it's possible, try to eat organic.

- Remember that low fat doesn't necessarily equate to healthy, our body needs some fats to function properly.

- Stick to complex carbohydrates (wholemeal bread, oatmeal, brown rice, fruit and vegetables), and stay away from simple carbohydrates (white bread, white rice, pasta and all refined sugars).

- Proteins are essential for amino acid intake and production, animal products and fish contain all the amino acids we require, but it is possible to get these from vegetarian options too.

- Ensure your vitamin and mineral intake is high and nothing is lacking. Also, keep hydrated and always try to filter your water if possible.

- Use the 80% alkaline and 20% acid rule for each meal to give your body the best chance to keep healthy.

- Preparation for having a baby can take up to a year, and even longer if your nutrition has been bad for some time. Be patient and think about how you're giving your baby the best start in life.

Chapter Four

Anti-fertility Factors

Toxic metals/heavy metals

All trace elements can become toxic in large quantities. However, the term 'toxic' usually applies to elements which are not recognised as having an essential function, and when accumulated in the body have a negative effect on normal functioning. In the context of this book, we are looking at metals which can have an adverse effect on fertility and these include:

- Mercury.
- Aluminium.
- Cadmium.
- Copper.
- Lead.

There is an assumption among government health departments, GPs, industry and the public that something is safe unless proved otherwise. When seeking maximum fertility, I suggest the reverse should be true, that potentially toxic substances should be considered dangerous to human function unless proved safe.

'When seeking maximum fertility, I suggest potentially toxic substances should be considered dangerous to human function unless proved safe.'

Mercury

This is one element where a body of research has identified hormone disruption due to mercury toxicity. There are three types of mercury: elemental, non-organic and organic. Organic mercury is slow to be eliminated from our bodies and poses the more serious problems.

Most if us have the ability to detoxify these heavy metals. Problems can occur when our immune system is not working as well as it should, or when the exposure to a toxic element is more than the immune system can deal with at a particular time. For example, if your body is fighting off an infection, that will be the priority for the immune system.

There are some people who appear to be particularly sensitive to small amounts of these substances, therefore if you are having a problem conceiving, my advice would be to try and avoid your exposure to these elements where possible. A simple hair analysis would discover any toxic overload. (See help list.)

Mercury is found in pesticides, fungicides, large fish (e.g. tuna) and dental fillings. High levels of mercury will affect your libido and both egg and sperm production.

Aluminium

Aluminium interferes with the absorption of other essential vitamins, seriously compromising nutritional and immune status which then poses a problem for fertility.

Aluminium is found in most underarm deodorants, antacid formulas, aluminium pans (particularly if used to cook acid fruits or green leafy vegetables) and some water supplies.

Cadmium

Cadmium is a common pollutant which will affect both fertility and pregnancy outcomes.

The main sources are cigarettes and processed food. There is a high cadmium to zinc ratio in white flour, this is because zinc in the germ bran layers is removed during the milling process, and cadmium is found mostly in the centre of the grain and is left untouched. When the zinc/cadmium ratio is left intact, as in wholegrain flour, cadmium loses its potential to disrupt enzyme activity. We are talking of minute amounts here which are not immediately harmful in normal healthy beings.

Copper

Copper is an essential mineral and only becomes toxic as levels rise uncontrollably. High copper will damage fertility, increase risk of miscarriage and possibly cause long-term problems with newborn infants.

Long-term use of the birth control pill or copper coils can cause copper levels to rise.

Lead

Lead is well documented as a harmful substance. Lead interferes with the normal functioning of other trace elements and causes a loss of valuable nutrients. Lead can affect the fertility of both men and women.

Men exposed to lead experience a fall in sperm count with sperms becoming malformed and hardly mobile. In women, high lead counts can be the sole cause of miscarriage, stillbirth and congenital abnormality of any surviving baby.

Often with a high lead count, the egg's implantation in the uterus does not occur as the uterine environment is not good enough for a nine-month settlement – essentially the body knows the pregnancy will fail and sends messages to prevent conception.

Alcohol

There is no known safe limit to the amount of alcohol that you can drink when planning a pregnancy or when you are pregnant. Therefore, it is safe to recommend no alcohol in the preconception preparation phase for both partners and during pregnancy for the woman.

Alcohol acts as a diuretic (encourages the production of urine) removing essential zinc from the kidneys causing an imbalance of the zinc:copper ratio.

Alcohol is rapidly absorbed into the bloodstream and carried to all parts of the body, including the brain. Sperm and egg production can be severely diminished by the presence of blood alcohol. Research has shown that alcohol

'Therefore, it is safe to recommend no alcohol in the preconception preparation phase for both partners and during pregnancy for the woman.'

has a specific effect on chromosomes (cells that carry our genetic material) and is a cause of miscarriage and of babies born with serious mental and physical handicap, this is described as foetal alcohol syndrome.

Men must refrain from drinking alcohol in the preparation phase. Alcohol affects sperm production and in heavy drinkers sperm abnormalities are more common, with sperm lacking normal tails with consequent reduced motility. Testosterone production is also reduced. Research has also shown that babies born to fathers who drink have a lowered birth weight.

Alcohol is also one of the main causes of male impotence.

Caffeine

We think of coffee for a caffeine fix, however, caffeine is present in tea, soft drinks, some foods and medicines. Caffeine has an initial stimulating effect which can temporarily relieve fatigue or mild depression. It also stimulates the kidneys and raises blood pressure. Caffeine is addictive and reducing intake can produce the same type of withdrawal symptoms as one would expect from any addictive substance. These include shivering, nightmares, loss of libido, insomnia and altered bowel habits.

Caffeine is classed as an anti-nutrient because it leaches B vitamins out of the body. Caffeine can affect your ability to conceive and your ability to carry a pregnancy to full term.

My advice would be for both partners to cut out caffeine as much as possible in preparation for pregnancy. There is sufficient evidence to support this.

Smoking

In recognition that smoking is harmful to health, the government has now made smoking in enclosed public places illegal. This should be sufficient warning for all would-be parents. However, just to reinforce this message it is worth noting that female smoking is linked to infertility, and babies born to smoking mothers have a lowered birth weight due to damage to the placenta caused by nicotine decreasing the amount of blood flow in the uterus. Heavy smokers and drinkers have a six times greater risk of stillbirth.

Social drugs

These include marijuana, cocaine, crack and heroin. For anyone with fertility problems these substances must be eliminated. These drugs lower fertility, are teratogenic (produce abnormalities) and have serious long-term effects on babies' growth and development.

Smoking marijuana is four times more dangerous than cigarette smoking and adversely affects both sperm and egg production.

If you are looking to these substances as an aid to relaxation, then alternatives must be found. Take up a sport, join a yoga or Pilates class or any kind of new activity which will allow diversion from your usual routine.

Medical drugs

As far as possible, avoid any kind of medication. Over-the-counter medicines, including ibuprofen, asprin and cold remedies, like all drugs, have an effect on the biochemistry of the body and should be taken with care. There are times when antibiotics may be necessary but they disrupt the normal flora in the gut which may, in turn, lead to reduced absorption of essential vitamins and minerals.

Some antidepressants decrease sperm count and motility. You may also find, once your mineral status has been corrected, your depression may no longer remain a problem.

Tranquillisers, painkilling drugs, including aspirin and paracetamol, anti-convulsant drugs and anti-hypertensive drugs can only be reduced under close supervision of a medical practitioner. Speak to your GP about possible ways of reducing any medication you're currently prescribed. Do not, under any circumstances, stop taking your prescription before consulting your GP.

Infections

Many of us are aware that certain infections can adversely affect the development of a foetus in the uterus, for example, rubella (German measles).

'Smoking marijuana is four times more dangerous than cigarette smoking and adversely affects both sperm and egg production.'

We also know, since the tragedy of thalidomide, that the placenta offers little in the way of a barrier to noxious substances as previously believed. In this section, we are looking at infections as an obstruction to conception.

Many genito-urinary infections, otherwise known as sexually transmitted infections (STIs), have few or no outward symptoms, making diagnosis difficult. In order to regain control of your fertility you cannot ignore this issue, even if you feel you are at little or no risk. For example, partners who are faithful to each other and have had minimal or no other sexual contact, can still be sharing a thrush (candida) infection. The female partner may have a vaginal discharge which is treated medically, but her partner, who is symptom free, will be reinfecting her unless he is treated at the same time.

There is little doubt that with the advent of the birth control pill and a more liberal society, both men and women have an increased number of partners during their reproductive life. This inevitably exposes each individual to a greater number of possible infected contacts. Do not be complacent over this issue.

Bacteria infections

Chlamydia

Chlamydia is caused by the bacteria Chlamydia trachomatis and is harmful to both men and women. Women may suffer from pelvic inflammatory disease (PID) and men from non-specific urethritis (NSU). Sadly, chlamydia can infect the reproductive system for a long time before any symptoms appear. It is a very common infection which rapidly spreads from vaginal, oral or anal sex.

Symptoms in women include an abnormal vaginal discharge, lower back pain, a burning sensation when passing urine, raised temperature, painful sex and disruption to periods. Men can have an abnormal discharge from the penis, a burning sensation when passing urine and itching around the genitals. Chlamydia is by far the most common STI; a self-testing kit is available from chemists as part of the National Chlamydia Screening Programme, see help list for more information.

If treated early, chlamydia can be completely cured with antibiotics.

Gonorrhoea

Gonorrhoea is caused by the bacteria neisseria gonorrhoeae-gonococcus and is highly infectious. It spreads from vaginal, oral or anal sex and has serious consequences upon fertility for both men and women, left untreated it can lead to sterility. Symptoms may be mild and mistaken for bladder infections. Treatment is with antibiotics.

Other bacterial infections

Bacteroids, haem Strep, haem influenza, Staph aureus and B. Streptococci are bacterial infections often present when other infections are diagnosed.

Symptoms may be mild or non-existent but any bacterial infection will compromise fertility and may be the single cause of miscarriage.

Viruses

Herpes

It is the herpes simplex virus which causes herpes. There are two types of virus – type 1 causes sores around the mouth and nose, commonly called cold sores. Type 2 is more severe and causes sores in the genital area of both men and women. The blisters are very painful and highly infective. The blisters can disappear but the infection remains. There is no absolute cure although antiviral drugs can help to keep the infection under control. Although it is possible to conceive and carry a baby to full term, the incidence of miscarriage is increased. If infection is visible when labour commences, a caesarean section will be advised to protect the baby from contact in the birth canal.

Cytomegalovirus

Cytomegalovirus is caused by one of the herpes viruses and is linked to a low sperm count in men and inflammation of the testes. It is also a cause of early miscarriage. Most people who are infected show no symptoms other than a feeling of tiredness and energy loss. Cytomegalovirus is passed from saliva and urine.

Hepatitis B

Hepatitis B is not just a sexually transmitted disease, as it can also be contracted from contact with body fluids, blood, saliva and urine. Hepatitis means inflammation of the liver but, like chlamydia and gonorrhoea, can be present without any severe symptoms. Treatment is slow requiring rest and good nutrition. Vaccination is available and it may become available more widely in the future if cases continue to rise.

AIDS

AIDS is caused by a retrovirus HIV, of which there are two types: HIV 1 and HIV 2. AIDS is transmitted by sexual contact, although it can be passed from shared syringes and needles in drug users. The HIV virus destroys white blood cells which are an important part of our immune defence, leaving the body open to infection with little natural resistance. Symptoms can take eight to 10 years to appear, so there is a long time when you can be a carrier without knowing.

Specialist antiviral drugs are used to treat this condition, relieve symptoms and prolong normal life. There is, at present, no cure.

Fungal infections

Thrush

Yeast (candida albicans) which occurs naturally in the body can cause problems when there is an overgrowth. The natural balance of bacteria and fungi can be altered by taking antibiotics or long-term use of the birth control pill or steroids. Chronic candidiasis can cause a range of symptoms, including gastro-intestinal upset, causing food allergies and sensitivities. Candida upsets the natural vaginal environment which then becomes hostile to in incoming sperm.

Treatment of both partners is essential with antifungal drugs and nutrition (removing all yeasts and sugars from the diet). A short course of vitamin A has been found to relieve some of the inflammation in the vagina and penis.

Flagellates

Trichomonas

Trichomonas is caused by the organism trichomonas and characterised in women by a profuse, itchy, smelly vaginal discharge which can be greenish in colour. It is very unlikely sperm will survive in this environment if sex is achieved at all. The vagina becomes very sore, making intercourse painful. In men, the penis becomes inflamed, particularly the area under the foreskin. Treatment is by a course of antibiotics for both partners.

Microscopic organisms

There are also microscopic organisms classified as mycoplasma, mycoplasma hominis and ureaplasma urealyticum, which are not exclusively spread by sexual contact, but nevertheless have been shown to reduce fertility. These organisms occur naturally in the reproductive tract but have been found in greater quantities in couples who are having problems conceiving. Their presence is completely symptomless, which is why testing is important.

Screening for these infective organisms is an essential part of your preconception work. It may be that your own GP is reluctant to refer you for these tests if you are not showing any symptoms of disease. Mention you have been trying unsuccessfully for a number of months or years to conceive and would like to rule out any hidden infection.

Visit a GUM clinic

'The best advice is to attend a GUM clinic at your local hospital or health clinic.'

The best advice is to attend a GUM clinic (genito-urinary medicine) at your local hospital or health clinic. These clinics are run by experienced doctors and nurses who have the correct equipment to carry out the necessary investigations on the spot. For some infections, results can be given immediately, for others you may have to wait one or two weeks for the results. This is a completely confidential service. You can self refer, so you do not need a GP's letter and the service is free on the NHS.

When you telephone the clinic to make an appointment, you will be given instructions prior to your appointment; for example, do not attend during menstruation as swabs will be taken from vagina and cervix.

For more information please see *Sexually Transmitted Infections – The Essential Guide* (Need2Know).

Summing Up

▨ As much as possible, try to avoid the toxic elements described in this chapter.

▨ Give up smoking and drinking alcohol in order to give conception the best possible chance of resulting in a pregnancy.

▨ It is absolutely essential to stop taking any illegal drugs in order to have a baby, there are serious consequences for babies' growth and development if you do not.

▨ Try to avoid prescribed medication, but speak to your GP about ways of doing this, do not, under any circumstances, stop taking a prescribed medication without consulting your GP first.

▨ Do not rule out the chance of an STI, go to your local GUM clinic to undergo the tests to ensure there are no STIs present.

Chapter Five

Female Infertility

There are no accurate figures that truly represent the incidence of infertility, although a number of studies suggest an increase in incidence over the last two decades. During the 1980s it was thought to be one in eight couples and today that figure is estimated at one in four for couples starting out on their first pregnancy.

Once more we can separate the problem from those women who have already conceived but with an unsuccessful outcome, from those women that have never conceived. In the former, we know the equipment is there but function inadequate, and in the latter we may have to embark upon further examinations.

For any woman wishing to conceive, it is recommended that her partner is checked out first. A sperm count is a relatively simple, non-invasive test. In the past women have subjected themselves to a number of invasive procedures, only to find that their partner had a low sperm count. At one time it was automatically assumed that infertility was exclusively a female problem. Times have changed, and we now know that infertility can affect both men and women equally and if both partners have a problem, then a return to reproductive health may take a little longer.

Causes of infertility, including women who are able to become pregnant but not carry the baby to full term are:

▓ Structural faults.

▓ Disorder of endocrine function (including early menopause).

▓ Endometriosis.

▓ Polycystic ovary syndrome (PCOS).

▓ Fibroids.

'For any woman wishing to conceive, it is recommended that her partner is checked out first. A sperm count is a relatively simple, non-invasive test.'

- Pelvic inflammatory disease (PID).

- Asherman's syndrome.

- Hughes syndrome.

- Factor V Leiden disorder.

- STIs and sexually aggravated infections.

- Acidic vaginal secretions.

- Toxic womb.

- Nutritional deficiencies.

- Body weight.

- Poor libido and/or painful sex.

Structural faults

'Having a full osteopathic examination is an essential part of pregnancy planning.'

The spinal column houses the spinal cord whose branches are the nerve centre of the body. Any spinal or pelvic displacement, which incidentally may not produce any severe symptoms or symptoms that are not recognised as being structural in origin, can have an effect on reproductive ability. Having a full osteopathic examination is an essential part of pregnancy planning.

However, some women may have some kind of congenital functional problem (i.e. one which they were born with), for example, this could be a complete absence of a uterus or small malfunctioning ovaries. These conditions only affect a minority of women whose only alternative is either a surrogate pregnancy with their partner's sperm or adoption. These conditions would be revealed by an ultrasound examination.

There are also women who have what is termed a 'bicornuate uterus', whereby the uterus is divided into two separate halves but joined with a common cervix. This is not necessarily a serious cause of infertility as the equipment is working, but there will be a lowered chance each month of a pregnancy. As we know, an egg is released from alternative ovaries each month, but, for example, if an egg is released from the right ovary but many sperm have located themselves in the left horn of the uterus, access to the all-important egg is denied. This condition often occurs in families but many women do not know they have the condition until they become pregnant and the baby is occupying only half of the abdomen. There are no problems attached to the outcome of such pregnancies which carry the same minimal risks as a normal pregnancy.

Structural abnormalities are revealed on ultrasound examination.

Fallopian tubes

A structural fault could also mean that the fallopian tubes are blocked, the common cause of this is infection (salpingitis), either as a result of long-term pelvic inflammatory disease or the silent nature of bacterial infections, including chlamydia. Blocked fallopian tubes account for 15% of all cases of infertility. If the infection has been eradicated and the fallopian tube only recently blocked (i.e. a short time the two sides of the tube have been stuck together) it may be possible to reverse the condition by good diet combined with corrective surgery.

Diagnosis is by hysterosalpingogram (HSG), this is an X-ray procedure usually performed in a day case unit under mild sedation. A vaginal speculum is used to open the vagina and a plastic or metal tube is inserted through the cervix into the uterus and injected with a liquid radiopaque dye, which will show clearly on an X-ray. If the liquid flows out of both tubes, then all is well, however if the dye gets stuck in one or both tubes, a diagnosis of blockage is made. The whole procedure is completed within half an hour.

Alternatively, a hysterosalpingosonogram (HSS) may be carried out. This procedure is very similar to HSG, but instead of using X-ray, the uterus and tubes are examined with the use of ultrasound.

In some cases a laparoscopy may be offered. This is a minimally invasive procedure which can give you and your doctor a lot of information. Performed under a mild anaesthetic in a day case unit, a small incision is made beneath your belly button and a laparoscope (telescope) inserted. The surgeon can then look through the laparoscope to see if one or both your tubes are open. The laparoscope can also be used to look for other problems which may be affecting your fertility, such as scar tissue or endometriosis (tissue from the lining of the uterus growing in the wrong place).

Surgery for reversal of sterilisation

Surgery for reversal of sterilisation is only performed in very special situations. Women now receive sufficient counselling prior to this procedure and are given much more information than in the past. However, occasionally through remarriage or loss of a much-loved child, some women embark upon this procedure but success is limited. The clip which has held the tube together is removed and the compressed area cut away and the tube surgically rejoined. Good nutrition will aid the healing process.

Damage to tubes following a tubal ectopic pregnancy

Occasionally the fertilised egg remains in the tube and does not make the journey into the uterus. This is a very serious condition as the tube is just not large enough to accommodate a rapidly developing embryo. The woman experiences severe abdominal pain and surgery to remove the embryo is essential. The fallopian tube may actually burst, known as a ruptured ectopic pregnancy, in which case the tube is damaged beyond repair.

There remains a working fallopian tube on the other side, so a pregnancy is still possible. A serious problem arises if a second ectopic pregnancy occurs in the remaining tube. Once the tubes are damaged in this way, in vitro fertilisation (IVF) is advised.

Disorder of endocrine function

There are a number of hormones circulating in the environment which we term exogenous (foreign hormones) and are present in the food chain. Foreign oestrogens have been linked to early onset of puberty and menstruation. A century ago, the average onset of menstruation was between 14 and 15 years of age, today we have seen that reduced, with girls as young as 8 and 9 years starting puberty and menstruation. Many mothers claim their daughters are being 'robbed' of their childhood. Sadly, early menopause may be another symptom.

Being overweight can also upset hormone balance as the fat cells produce oestrogen which is in excess of normal requirements. It's important to reach and maintain a healthy weight for your height to minimise hormone imbalance.

We must also look at digestive problems and liver function which are uniquely united in hormone balance. The activities of both our gut (digestive system) and liver have a direct connection with the amount of oestrogen circulating in the blood.

Oestrogen is broken down in the intestines and is co-ordinated by the liver. If this process is interrupted, either by malfunction of the gut or liver, you will have a higher level than normal of oestrogen circulating. As a result, your body keeps getting the wrong signals on which hormone to release.

Hormone control is dependent upon the body working efficiently and the health of our body is dependent upon an efficient digestive system. If we are not eating health-giving foods or our gut is unable to absorb nutrients, then our ability to reproduce is severely compromised. If you have any food allergies or sensitivity, are mildly depressed or suffer from headaches, and have taken courses of antibiotics, it may be the balance of the special bacteria that live in your gut has been disturbed. The term dysbiosis describes this condition. It is also a major cause of an overgrowth of fungi (Candida) in the gut.

There are simple rules to follow when healing the gut and they are known as 'the four Rs':

- Remove – take away anything that will irritate the gut, for example alcohol, drugs, parasites (not uncommon) and foods high in refined sugar.

- Re-inoculate – take a course of pre and probiotics.

- Replace – it may be necessary to add back digestive enzymes for a short period.

- Repair – take a course of essential amino acid, L Glutamine.

Internal Parasites

A parasitic infection of the gut may be symptomless, but the parasite is competing with natural bugs in the gut for dominance, causing an imbalance in nutrients. If your GP, naturopath or nutritional therapist believe a parasitic

'It's important to reach and maintain a healthy weight for your height to minimise hormone imbalance.'

infection exists, then they will recommend an examination of your stool which can be done simply under the NHS. Stool tests can also be performed privately (see help list).

A healthy gut is essential to good hormone balance. A registered naturopath or nutritional therapist will be able to guide you through this programme (see help list).

Assessment of your hormone levels will be done via blood, urine and saliva tests.

Endometriosis

Endometriosis is inflammation of the endometrium, or lining of the uterus, with implantation of endometrial cells outside the uterus itself. This is a very painful and distressing condition affecting 10-15% of women between the ages of 24-45 and severely affecting their fertility. Endometrial cells can migrate into the fallopian tubes, ovary, vagina, bladder and bowel. These endometrial cells respond in the same way as the endometrial cells in the uterus and bleed in response to the normal hormonal cycle of menstruation. The problem is, unlike the uterus where the blood flows naturally through the cervix and out into the vagina, there is nowhere for the blood to flow from abnormal sites. This causes severe pain and scarring of the tissue.

Tampons are thought to cause a backflow of blood when inserted at night and a link with endometriosis has been suggested. Regular changing of tampons is recommended to reduce infection risk, as is the use of natural, chlorine-free tampons.

Treatment will be dependent upon how severe the symptoms are. Under the expert care of a gynaecologist, drugs may be used initially in an attempt to shrink the endometrial tissue. In very severe cases a hysterectomy may be offered. This operation must not be undertaken without adequate counselling, particularly if the woman wishes to have a pregnancy.

Before undertaking a hysterectomy you should try natural treatments first, including healing the gut as already mentioned and making specific dietary changes.

Polycystic ovary syndrome (PCOS)

This can be a confusing condition both in diagnosis and understanding.

The word 'syndrome' indicates the condition is a collection of differing signs and symptoms. During the normal menstrual cycle, immature eggs are stimulated in a ripening process ready for release. These eggs are encapsulated in a Graafian follicle and when they reach maturity are released and captured by the finger-like ends of the fallopian tubes. This process is termed 'ovulation'. The remaining follicles wither and die. In PCOS, the follicles do not wither but remain as multiple cysts covering the ovary.

In mild cases, you may not be aware that you have PCOS. However, in severe cases fertility is seriously compromised due to hormone imbalance. Periods may be irregular or stop altogether and hair growth on the face, breasts and inside of the legs is particularly stressful.

Diagnosis is made by taking blood tests to determine hormone levels and by ultrasound examination. Your doctor may recommend a short course of medication in an attempt to normalise hormone levels.

Fibroids

Fibroids are growths that appear in the muscle layer (myometrium) of the uterus and are sometimes known as myomas. They occur commonly in the 35 to 50 age group and often disappear after the menopause when oestrogen production is greatly reduced. They do not always interfere with fertility particularly if they are only small, however, as they grow, and depending upon where they are situated in the uterus, implantation of the fertilised egg may be difficult. Fibroids often occur in families, so if your mother had fibroids, you are more likely to develop them.

Problems also arise as periods are longer and heavier. Anaemia (loss of the red blood cells) may result, further compromising fertility.

Diagnosis is made by vaginal examination or by pelvic ultrasound. Treatment depends upon their size and symptoms but will be either by drugs or surgery.

Pelvic inflammatory disease (PID)

We have already mentioned how infections can greatly reduce your chance of becoming pregnant. If left untreated, irreparable damage can be done to the reproductive organs. In particular, the fallopian tubes become inflamed and blocked with devastating consequences. Any untreated sexually transmitted disease can cause PID.

Symptoms include pelvic pain, high temperature, foul-smelling vaginal discharge and a stinging pain when passing urine.

Asherman's syndrome

Asherman's syndrome affects approximately 3,500 women each year and is thought to be the cause of 5% of infertility cases. Sadly, this condition is often misdiagnosed. It is caused by scar tissue forming inside the uterus as a result of a surgical procedure including dilation and curettage (D&C) – this can happen following surgical removal of fibroids.

Asherman's can cause infertility and miscarriage. Diagnosis is made by looking inside the uterus by HSG examination or hysteroscopy.

Anyone with a history of operative procedures on the uterus who fails to become pregnant or suffers from repeated miscarriage, should ask their doctor to examine them for this condition.

Treatment is by hysteroscopic sugery where fine scissors cut away the scar tissue and then the uterus is filled with water, or a balloon or coil inserted, to keep the uterus open and prevent further scar formation. This procedure is usually successful in the hands of an experienced surgeon.

Hughes syndrome

This condition is also known as antiphospholipid syndrome, or APS, and sometimes 'sticky blood'. It was first discovered in 1983 when Dr Hughes was looking at patients with autoimmune problems and discovered many of his patients had suffered from recurrent miscarriages. Hughes syndrome can be diagnosed by a simple blood test to detect antibodies which cause the blood to become 'sticky', thus reducing the blood flow which is required to sustain a pregnancy.

Treatment is by a daily dose of aspirin or some other anticoagulant to thin the blood. Naturopathic measures would be to eat a diet rich in anticoagulant properties, for example, garlic and magnesium-containing foods such as green vegetables, oily fish and evening primrose oil.

Factor V Leiden disorder

Factor V Leiden disorder is also known as activated protein C resistance. This is another blood disorder similar to Hughes syndrome, the collective term of which are 'coagulopathies' (meaning blood that tends to clot more easily). Women who carry the gene for Factor V Leiden disorder, have an increased risk of miscarriage and stillbirth due to clotting in the placenta. Some women who carry the gene will complete a pregnancy without any problems, whereas others have repeated miscarriages and/or deep vein thrombosis (clots forming, usually in the legs) within weeks of a pregnancy.

Treatment is similar to that of Hughes syndrome, with blood-thinning drugs.

Like Hughes syndrome, most women are initially misdiagnosed. If you have a history of blood clotting in your family or have suffered from a number of miscarriages, then ask your GP to test your blood for this condition.

Sexually transmitted infections

Please see chapter 4 for information on sexually transmitted infections.

Acidic vaginal secretions

The vagina is slightly more acidic than the rest of the body. This is because the vagina is an open door to the inside of the pelvis. Invading organisms are deterred by the acidic environment and the unwanted invaders are prevented from multiplying. The vagina also produces specialist organisms called Doderlein's bacillus which help to maintain the protective acidity of the vagina.

Occasionally the vagina can become too acidic and leads to an incompatibility with the deposited sperm. We will discuss this in more detail in chapter 8.

Toxic womb

'PCBs are a family of over 200 compounds used in the manufacture of electronic equipment.'

This has become a popular term as we enter the 21st century. Manmade chemicals including such compounds as dioxin, polychlorinated biphenyls (PCBs) and the pesticide DDT, have found their way into our food chain and left residues in our fat cells. There are also incidences of heavy metal toxicity with traces of lead, cadmium, mercury, aluminium and copper found contaminating our tissues. Our bodies are not used to eliminating the contaminants of the 20th century and toxicity results. Simply put, it is likened to putting a baby into a 'dirty bed'. Preparation for pregnancy should include reducing toxicity and be as natural and routine as cleaning our teeth.

Adopting an organic diet, replacing any lost minerals, healing our digestive system and taking care of your liver will all combine to help eliminate or 'detox' your body of unwanted substances.

Dr Michel Odent has pioneered a detox system for pre-pregnancy which he calls the 'accordion method'. We all have up to 500 differing synthetic chemicals in our body which would not have been there 50 years ago. Most of these chemicals are stored in fat cells waiting for an opportunity to be removed from the system.

There are a number of chemicals which concern us as we attempt to overcome infertility:

- Dioxins – dioxins encompass a family of 219 chlorinated chemicals produced as waste from many industrial processes. We are all exposed to dioxins through our diet.

- PCBs – PCBs are a family of over 200 compounds used in the manufacture of electronic equipment.

- Trans fatty acids – to make a vegetable oil firm for spreading, a hydrogen ion is passed through the oil to achieve a coagulation effect, it is during this process a trans fat is produced which is why low-fat and polyunsaturated margarines should be avoided. A trans fat is a non-nutrient.

Dr Odent's accordion programme seeks to mobilise fat-soluble pollutants which the body will then eliminate via the bowel, urine, skin and breath. It is a seven-day exercise which encompasses short, fast drinks rich in vitamins and minerals, exercise and hot steam baths. At the end of the session, women are encouraged to have a short two-day fast once a month prior to conception. For more information, see help list.

Nutritional deficiencies

Even if you are eating a healthy, organic diet, you may still be lacking in certain nutrients. For example, long-term use of the birth control pill lowers zinc levels and increases copper. Some intrauterine contraceptive devices (IUDs) can also increase copper levels. Dental fillings or canal root work can increase mercury. Remember also, that as a result of modern methods of farming, fruits and vegetables have lost some of their previous high levels of minerals and vitamins. See chapter 3 for more information on fertility and diet.

'Even if you are eating a healthy, organic diet, you may still be lacking in certain nutrients.'

Body weight

Women who are seriously underweight or seriously overweight, may have problems conceiving. Being underweight with a body mass index (BMI) of less than 18.4, can cause ovulation to cease and is an indication of poor nutrition. BMI is calculated by dividing your weight in kilograms by the square of your height in meters. Women who have suffered from anorexia and or bulimia have reduced stores of essential vitamins and minerals, they are often not ovulating due to hormone disruption caused by the eating disorder and a lack of essential fats in their diet. Women who religiously adopt a low-fat diet also risk anovulation (not ovulating). Fat is an essential component of a healthy diet.

Overweight women, with a BMI of more than 29, statistically take longer to conceive. Fat cells produce small amounts of oestrogen, which, if you are very overweight, could lead to having too much oestrogen, stopping ovulation. Being overweight may be linked to PCOS.

Men who are either overweight or underweight can also become infertile with a reduced sperm count and poor sperm quality.

Poor libido and/or painful sex

'Illness and depression reduce sex drive so it is important to get a correct diagnosis, poor libido may be a symptom of your illness, or a side effect of treatment you are receiving.'

There are a number of complex reasons why we either find sex distasteful or painful which we will discuss in more detail in chapter 8.

However, wanting a baby does not always equate with good sex, nor is it necessary to orgasm at the same time, although the two fit together very well.

Illness and depression reduce sex drive so it is important to get a correct diagnosis, poor libido may be a symptom of your illness, or a side effect of treatment you are receiving. Thyroid disease can adversely affect your desire for sex.

Summing Up

- For any woman wishing to conceive, it is recommended that her partner is checked out first, a sperm count is a relatively simple, non-invasive test.

- Lots of factors can affect fertility, some are purely medical and some can be a snowball effect of lifestyle and diet factors all combining to create a condition where pregnancy is difficult to achieve.

- Try to eat as healthily as possible, using organic produce and products to aid healthy digestion, vitamin and mineral intake and maintain a healthy weight for optimum health when trying to conceive.

- Find a gynaecologist who specialise in investigating fertility problems, they will do an exhaustive investigation to find out the root of the problem.

Chapter Six

Male Infertility

At one time it was thought infertility was entirely a female problem and many women endured years of various investigations, when in actual fact it was their partner who had a problem. Male infertility counts for approximately 40% of infertility between couples.

Semen is the fluid ejaculated from the penis at sexual climax. The semen contains up to 500 million sperms suspended in a fluid secreted by the prostate gland and seminal vesicles. On ejaculation the semen is very sticky, greyish in colour and measures about 2ml or about half a teaspoon.

To prepare the sperm for rapid movement, the semen quickly becomes more watery once in the vagina, providing a more protective alkaline medium in which the sperm can swim. The semen contains a sugar substance to give the sperm energy along their tortuous journey through the cervix, uterus and finally the fallopian tube.

Causes of infertility in men are:

- Low sperm count (oligozoospermia).
- Absence of live sperm in the semen (azoospermia).
- Poor movement of the sperm in the semen (asthenozoospermia).
- Unhealthy, abnormal sperm.
- Antisperm antibodies.
- Structural/congenital problems
- Retrograde ejaculation.
- Hormones, cholesterol and stress.
- Cancer.
- Impotence.

Low sperm count

This is usually the first investigation and although the test is simple and non-invasive, it can cause embarrassment. Collection is through masturbation which can be done in a private room within the clinic where there is access to soft porn magazines. Alternatively, if the ejaculate can be delivered to the laboratory within one hour you could do this at home.

Normal sperm count is 60 to 80 million per 1ml of semen. Below 20 million, fertility is compromised. A count less than 5 million sperm is classed as being infertile.

Causes of temporary low sperm count:

- Excess use of alcohol, tobacco and social drugs, including marijuana.

- Prescription drugs.

- Stress and lack of sleep.

- Increased scrotal temperature.

- Exposure to radiation, solvents and pesticides.

- Infections, including the common cold and flu.

'You can take control of sperm production by avoiding alcohol, tobacco and social drugs.'

You can take control of sperm production by:

- Avoiding alcohol, tobacco and social drugs.

- Asking your GP to check out any prescribed medication you are taking to ensure it does not interfere with sperm production.

- Incorporating time for yourself during the week to help with stress and lack of sleep. Many men now take up yoga or Tai Chi, as an aid to stress reduction.

- Maintaining a normal scrotal temperature, which is 94-96°F, or 34-35°C, above this temperature sperm production stops. Men are advised to avoid wearing tight-fitting pants, to wear loose cotton boxer shorts and to allow the testicles to hang free whenever possible. To aid the normal temperature, use a cold shower on the testicles and when driving long distances, take a flask of iced water and pour over the testicles at regular intervals. Also, avoid exercises which increase scrotal temperature, like treadmills and jogging.

- Reducing laptop use – research has shown that men who want a family should not rest a laptop computer on their thighs. In just 15 minutes a laptop can raise the temperature of the scrotum by one degree centigrade, sufficient to reduce the live sperm count by 40% as well as damaging any surviving sperm, 60 minutes of use can wipe out all live sperm.

- Avoiding exposure to radiation, solvents and pesticides – eat organic foods whenever possible, avoid processed foods, hydrogenated fats, trans fatty acids and refined sugar. Try to identify and eliminate any environmental pollutants, many underarm deodorants contain aluminium which is readily absorbed from the soft, porous underarm skin. There are various nutritional supplements which may be helpful, seek the advice of a nutrition specialist. Also, try to avoid dietary sources of oestrogens and long absences of ejaculation.

- Stay in good health to avoid picking up colds and germs from others.

Absence of live sperm in the semen

This is quite a rare occurrence and requires blood tests to investigate hormone activity. It may be necessary to perform a testicular biopsy. In some cases your fertility specialist may call in the advice of a senior urologist as there may be a functional problem with the prostate gland.

Poor movement of the sperm in the semen

At least 50% of the sperm should be moving rapidly. The energy and the ability of the sperm to swim forward is essential to conception. Regular ejaculation assists the movement of sperm as motility is impaired when they have been in storage for a length of time.

During analysis your sperm will be given a graded scale:

- Rapid movement, sperm swimming strongly and in straight lines.

- Slow progression where movement is in short spurts.

- No movement forward, although sperm are obviously alive.

- Completely no movement with large numbers of inactive sperm.

'Research has shown that men who want a family should not rest a laptop computer on their thighs. In just 15 minutes a laptop can raise the temperature of the scrotum by one degree centigrade.'

Unhealthy, abnormal sperm

Morphology is the term given to looking at the size and shape of the sperm. If there are large numbers of abnormal sperm (e.g. sperm with no tails, no heads or completely abnormal in some way) then fertilisation of an egg is an impossibility. The WHO state a minimum of 15% normal sperms must be present in any one sample to be sure of fertility.

If you are reading this and have been told you have a low sperm count with a number of abnormal sperm, do not despair as raising sperm count is a possibility with the correct advice and treatment. Adopting the lifestyle changes as previously discussed will greatly enhance both the amount and quality of your sperm.

Sperm DNA fragmentation assay (SDFA)

This is a relatively new test for diagnosing abnormal sperm and an important one, particularly for couples who have had numerous attempts at assisted conception without any success.

The test evaluates the quality of the DNA (genetic material) contained in each sperm. The primary function of sperm is to deliver DNA to the egg to enable the complex formation of an embryo. It is therefore important that good quality DNA is delivered to the egg to ensure positive pregnancy success.

The standard semen analysis provides information on the count, motility (movement) and morphology (quality) of the sperm but does not assess what is being delivered in terms of DNA. Men with otherwise normal semen analysis can have a high degree of DNA damage and men with what was thought to be a poor sperm count can have sperms with very good DNA. By testing for DNA fragmentation many previously unexplained failures with assisted conception treatments can now be understood.

A normal sample will contain sperm with less than 15% fragmentation damage. DNA damaged sperm that are in numbers of above 30%, the advice would be not to proceed with infertility treatment until there is an improvement in sperm quality.

It can be hard to maintain a positive mind when faced with such evidence. However, it is important to remember that you are in the driving seat and that with support from an experienced infertility practitioner and your willingness to incorporate lifestyle changes, even this unhappy situation has every chance of being reversed.

Postcoital test

This test measures the ability of sperm to survive the hostile acid environment of the vagina and their ability to penetrate the cervical mucus after intercourse. Obviously the female partner has to attend the clinic as soon after intercourse as is possible, usually at a pre-booked appointment, which can also prove an inhibiting factor to successful lovemaking. If the secretions in the vagina are too acidic, many of the sperm will die before reaching the entrance to the cervix.

Remember, if the majority of sperm are abnormal or lacking sufficient movement despite a normal sperm count, then it will be impossible to father a child unless there is an improvement in sperm health. A low sperm count but with healthy sperm does not always mean the man is infertile.

Antisperm antibodies

Antisperm antibodies are sometimes produced by the man against his own sperm, attacking the tail to make them immobile. This can happen following surgery for hernia repair or even after a vasectomy reversal whereby some sperm tissue has entered the bloodstream and set up an immune response. In other words, the body now recognises sperm as an invader. This immune response can also cause the sperm to stick together (agglutination).

Antibodies found in the sperm can also indicate a past or present infection of the male reproductive organs.

Antibody tests are not part of routine NHS investigations but may be done if there are indications that this could be the problem. Many private clinics do the antibody tests routinely.

Structural/congenital problems

Congenital simply means 'from birth'. Most congenital abnormalities are noticeable at birth, but some, for example Klinefelter's syndrome, only become apparent as adults. Congenital abnormalities are either inherited from one or both parents or are caused by some exposure to an environmental factor during development in the womb.

Klinefelter's syndrome

'Congenital simply means 'from birth'. Most congenital abnormalities are noticeable at birth, but some, for example Klinefelter syndrome, only become apparent as adults.'

Usually men will have an X and a Y chromosome (XY) and a woman, two X chromosomes (XX), but about one in 500 men are born with an extra X chromosome (XXY). These men have normal sex lives and do not find out they have an extra X chromosome until they discover they are infertile with no sperms in the semen.

Hypospadias

Hypospadias is where the opening of the urethra is underneath the penis, this is not uncommon but in most cases can be corrected surgically during infancy. However, if the opening is under the tip of the penis, it may go undetected until examination as an adult.

This condition does not impair sexual function but deposits semen in a less favourable place, lower in the vagina, which may slow down sperm movement through the cervix.

Undescended testicles

We understand the testicles hang loose from the body to keep cool. When the testicles have not dropped, we call this undescended. During foetal development the testicles are formed inside the body and proceed downwards through a small passage or canal to the outside. This process can be slow and the appearance of the testicles can take up to three months after birth. However, this condition may have gone undetected and examination of the testicles should be part of any investigation into infertility.

Need2Know

Varicoceles

A varicocele is a cluster of large dilated veins that drain blood away from the testicles. It is normal to have large prominent veins in this area so diagnosis may go undetected. The testicles should be examined whilst standing, for as soon as you lie down the blood drains away. Varicoceles are symptom-free apart from an occasional aching discomfort and only cause infertility in a small percentage of men. It is thought that the increased blood supply raises the temperature in the scrotum and therefore causes a reduction in sperm production and quality.

Surgical correction (varicocelectomy) usually results in a considerable improvement in sperm count, quality and motility.

Congenital absence of the vas deferens (CBAVD)

CBAVD is when a man's semen sample turns out to have no sperm cells, there is about a 2% risk of this being a problem. Until the advent of IVF, these men were unable to father a child, but it is now possible to retrieve sperm cells surgically for fertilisation.

Retrograde ejaculation

During ejaculation the semen is pulsated out from the penis, retrograde ejaculation is the opposite, that is, the semen is pulsated backwards into the bladder. This is a result of injury, either following a surgical procedure or by direct injury to the scrotal area and scar tissue has subsequently formed. It can also occur from any damage to the nervous system from spinal cord injuries or multiple sclerosis. This condition is discovered on clinical X-ray examination and can be reversed in most cases.

Hormones, cholesterol and stress

Everyday stresses become exaggerated with the additional concern over infertility. The body manages stress by increasing the production of stress hormones, cortisol and corticosterone, which are made from cholesterol in the adrenal glands. Sex hormones are made from the same material and use the same biochemical pathways. If stress levels continue to increase and the body is forced into producing increasing amounts of stress hormones, then production of sex hormones is diminished.

The problem is compounded if there are nutritional deficiencies as hormone production requires a number of essential vitamins and minerals. Stress uses up and diverts nutrients from sex hormone production.

To counteract this you should learn how to relax. Take plenty of exercise, meditate, eat good, organic, nutrient-rich foods and put variety into your life. Remember you are in the driving seat so take control of your emotions and lifestyle.

'The body manages stress by increasing the production of stress hormones. Sex hormones are made from the same material so if stress levels continue to increase production of sex hormones is diminished.'

Cancer

Some types of cancer produce a rise in body temperature or may produce abnormal hormones which temporarily interfere with sperm production. These cancers include testicular cancer, leukaemia, lymphoma and Hodgkin's disease. Many men in this situation will be advised to store their sperm as an insurance measure, although sperm production can return to normal once cancer treatment has been completed.

Often, the infertility problem is as a direct result of chemotherapy or radiation treatment.

Impotence

The lack of sexual drive or the inability to maintain an erection can be from deep emotional trauma, in this case careful professional counselling is required. The longer the problem exists, the feelings of loss and emasculation will be exaggerated. A deep sense of inadequacy can be a result of enormous stress at work or at home, with feelings of guilt, worthlessness, confusion and fear of losing their partner all adding up to make the problem appear insurmountable.

A loving and understanding partner can do much to relieve the situation. Relaxation, meditation and patience are required to resolve the situation.

Summing Up

- There can be several explanations for male infertility, including problems with sperm (amount, movement and quality), structural and congenital problems and emotional problems.

- Take control of your sperm count by giving up smoking, drinking and taking drugs. Speak to your GP about any prescription drugs you have been advised to take – could they be impairing your sperm production?

- Speak to an infertility specialist and get your sperm tested for the amount, movement and quality, there are also tests to check the quality of the sperm DNA.

- A range of structural or congenital issues could be causing infertility, speak to your specialist about any of those listed being a possibility.

- Hormones, cholesterol and stress can cause the production of sex hormones to reduce – take time to relax, exercise regularly and eat well to avoid this happening.

Chapter Seven

Blood Tests

Blood tests are essential to investigate the causes of infertility. There are a number of tests recommended to establish hormone levels and function and other tests which will examine your immune function and general health. Blood tests can be performed by your GP if they agree to investigate your infertility. Be prepared to discuss the blood tests with your GP, as many are available on the NHS.

Blood tests can become very costly when performed at a private clinic, but not all blood tests are readily available from the NHS and you should be aware of this.

Blood tests will be taken from both partners as hormone balance and assessment is not just a female issue.

'Blood tests can become very costly when performed at a private clinic, but not all blood tests are readily available from the NHS and you should be aware of this.'

Follicle-stimulating hormone (FSH)

Female

This test is done at the beginning of your menstrual cycle on days 2, 3 or 4. FSH is released by the pituitary gland and stimulates the growth of the ovarian follicles which will eventually release an egg. A low count is normal but as the level rises, this indicates that the ovaries are requiring higher levels of FSH to function. This test will give an indication of the quality and quantity of the eggs.

Male

FSH is essential for sperm development. If the FSH is high it may indicate testicular failure.

Luteinising hormone (LH)

Female

This test is also done at the beginning of the menstrual cycle on either day 2, 3 or 4. LH is controlled by the pituitary gland to stimulate ovulation and eventually the release of progesterone. A high blood level of LH is associated with polycystic ovary syndrome.

Male

LH stimulates the production of testosterone required for healthy sperm. High LH with a low testosterone indicates testicular failure which can be confirmed by biopsy.

Testosterone

Female

Although a male hormone, testosterone is also present in women. If the female testosterone level is high it can also be an indicator of polycystic ovary syndrome or a general hormone imbalance.

Male

Testosterone level is governed by the presence of LH so the blood test will be part of an overall hormone assessment. Levels alter during the day, being at their highest early morning. Timing of the blood test must be taken into consideration.

Oestradiol

Testing for oestradiol is part of the female investigations. This test is done at the same time as FSH and if the reading is high it may be an indicator of PCOS.

Anti-Mullerian hormone (AMH)

This test has received some publicity recently, as it is thought to be the best test to establish age-related decline in reproductive function, however, it is not routinely offered on the NHS. It is performed on day 3 of the menstrual cycle and a high concentration of AMH is a good indicator of a healthy supply of eggs.

AMH is produced by the ovarian follicles, so an abnormally high reading may be associated with polycystic ovaries found in some women with a difficulty in conceiving.

This test is also useful prior to IVF as an indicator of how well the ovaries will respond to stimulation.

Prolactin

Prolactin is secreted by the pituitary gland and its main function is to control the production of milk from the breasts after giving birth. During lactation prolactin levels are very high to suppress ovulation and protect the mother from another pregnancy. High prolactin in a non-lactating woman, can also prevent ovulation. It also regulates the production of progesterone and is therefore an important indicator of hormone balance.

Prolactin production is increased under stress which must be taken into account when interpreting the results.

Thyroid function tests

Thyroid disease is not uncommon and any disturbance with thyroid function can have an effect on fertility. Thyroid hormones are also produced by the pituitary gland and control all the essential activities in the body. A sluggish or underactive thyroid will reduce sexual performance. Severe symptoms of an underactive thyroid can produce impotence in men and anovulation (no ovulation) in women. This is an important additional test.

Rubella (German measles)

Although this test is carried out routinely in antenatal clinics, it is important to establish your immunity prior to becoming pregnant. If you are not immune and contract the infection during the first three months of pregnancy, there is a strong possibility the virus will cause severe abnormalities to the baby.

Vitamin D test

'Vitamin D is emerging as a crucial nutrient for women, particularly for women of childbearing age, as vitamin D is essential for the development of baby bones and reduces the risk of low birth weight babies.'

This is not a test offered routinely, except in some private clinics. Vitamin D is emerging as a crucial nutrient for women, particularly for women of childbearing age, as vitamin D is essential for the development of baby bones and reduces the risk of low birth weight babies. The Department of Health recommends vitamin D supplementation during pregnancy. The main source of vitamin D is from sunlight, so it may not be so surprising that vitamin D levels in many UK women tested were woefully low.

Vitamin D deficiency is easy to correct with specific supplementation, but all the published evidence for vitamin D recommends correction prior to pregnancy.

Summing Up

■ There are a variety of blood tests that can be carried out to find the possible causes of infertility. Not all of them will be available on the NHS and paying for private care can become costly.

■ Check you are immune to German measles.

■ Vitamin D deficiency is easy to diagnose and treat.

■ Thyroid function tests are an important addition to the pre-fertility work-up.

■ An anti-mullerian hormone test is useful to measure the number of remaining eggs.

Need2Know

Chapter Eight

Intercourse, Libido and Emotional Issues

Painful intercourse

Common sense tells us, if something is painful, then do not do it. This is not an option when planning a pregnancy, as regular sex is important and should be pleasurable for both partners. It is also a difficult topic to discuss even with your GP; and yet this may be the only barrier to a successful pregnancy and must be thoroughly investigated. Resolving painful sex will undoubtedly improve your chances of a pregnancy. The pain may be superficial from the area around the genitals or a deep pelvic pain.

Superficial pain is often from a bacterial or viral infection, such as chlamydia. Pain can be experienced on the tip of the penis or in and around the vulval area in women.

Painful intercourse in men

Painful intercourse in men may be caused by a congenital abnormality, for example a bowed erection (chordee) or a very tight foreskin (phimosis), both of which can be corrected with medical intervention. Inflammation of the prostate gland (prostatitis) will cause a sharp stabbing pain from the tip of the penis and may cause a widespread pelvic ache or a burning sensation on arousal and ejaculation.

Occasionally, a circumcision performed during infancy leaves some scar tissue which causes tightness at the tip of the penis during erection. This must be surgically corrected.

Some men suffer from a chronic inflammation and irritation of the foreskin making intercourse very painful. Circumcision will solve this problem. Adult circumcision will also be necessary if the foreskin does not pull back smoothly to allow a comfortable erection. Uncircumcised men must be very particular about hygiene, pulling back the foreskin when washing to avoid infection.

Painful intercourse in women

Insufficient vaginal lubrication will lead to discomfort for both partners. There are a number of reasons why this may happen, the important thing is to relax and enjoy foreplay, tell your partner what 'turns you on' and experiment different positions and techniques with each other. Vaginal lubricants can enhance intimacy, resolve dryness and restore comfort and ease to lovemaking. However, some conventional lubricants on the market are not sperm-friendly and inhibit the movement of sperm through the vagina. Always check any lubricant you use is organic and formulated especially to aid fertility.

'Any pain on intercourse must be thoroughly investigated.'

Psychosexual dysfunction can be due to an unconscious fear of intercourse. For example, vaginismus, a condition where the muscles of the vagina go into spasm preventing insertion of the penis, is usually psychological in origin. There are experienced counsellors available who are highly professional and can help you sort through these problems. Ask your GP or practice nurse who they would recommend in your area.

Deep pain on intercourse is frequently caused by pelvic problems, such as fibroids, ovarian cysts, endometriosis or pelvic inflammatory disease. Cystitis, or inflammation of the bladder, can also cause extreme discomfort. Any pain on intercourse must be thoroughly investigated.

Loss of libido

A loss of interest in sex can happen quite suddenly and is often a result of extreme stress and tiredness, sometimes it can be caused by a side effect of prescribed medication. For some couples who have been trying for many years to conceive, one or both partners may have lost the joy of sex along the journey. Remember there are five stages to arousal:

- Desire.
- Excitement.
- Plateau.
- Orgasm.
- Resolution.

Discuss these stages together in an attempt to reignite your passion for each other. Psychosexual therapy could help guide you through this process, see the help list for more details.

Best position

Actually, there is no particular position which is best for conception. The most important thing is that you are relaxed and enjoying the experience. Following intercourse, some women lie down with their feet in the air. There is no research to back this up, but my own view is, that if you want to try this, then put a pillow under your buttocks to give extra elevation of the pelvis. In theory this should aid sperm on their upward journey.

'There is no particular position which is best for conception. The most important thing is that you are relaxed and enjoying the experience.'

Emotional issues

Infertility is a huge emotional see-saw for both men and women. For committed couples this is a shared problem, an intensely intimate and private issue that must be faced together. It is a natural need to procreate, particularly in a loving relationship when a child is the longed for demonstration of both love and desire.

Once you have begun on the road to improving your diet and lifestyle and are charting your cycle, then do give yourselves time to relax together, enjoy your lovemaking and try to avoid becoming so engulfed by the desire to reproduce that the joy of sex is forgotten. This kind of scenario, when every intercourse is dominated by conquering infertility, will eventually lead to stress and division in your relationship. Stress produces hormones which are counterproductive to those hormones which are essential for reproduction, so relax and know that you will conceive.

Visualisation is an important tool. There is a body of evidence from biophysics demonstrating how what we think has a direct impact on our biochemistry.

When I am lecturing on this subject, I often say 'thoughts are things', what I am really saying is that negative thinking produces a negative influence within your body chemistry. Thinking, 'I am never going to get pregnant', or 'I am never going to be able to produce a child', gives your body that particular message. This is neither rocket science nor whimsical thinking, it is fact, 'thoughts are things', so please mentally congratulate your body and visualise yourself ovulating and becoming pregnant, or visualise healthy sperm being produced and your partner becoming pregnant. Believe a pregnancy is possible and visualise yourself holding your baby. I cannot overstress the benefits of visualisation, just try to do it, visualisation costs nothing but benefits are certainly possible.

Try to find time to meditate and focus on yourself, not the overwhelming desire for a baby. Anxiety increases sexual dysfunction.

For those couples said to be suffering from 'subfertility' or 'unspecific infertility', they really must relax. The best advice would be to go on holiday and forget all about baby-making, give each other time and allow nature to decide when and where.

Depression

Clinical depression is not uncommon after years of trying to conceive and perhaps a number of failed medical interventions. Your GP may prescribe antidepressant drugs, which will help relieve symptoms in the short term, but are not desirable for long-term use as they may reduce fertility and cause developmental damage to an unborn baby. Acupuncture has been proved to relieve symptoms of depression and is discussed later in this chapter.

Group therapy

Although infertility may be difficult to talk about within your own social group, it may be easier to talk with couples in the same situation. Research in America has shown that group psychological intervention with infertile women produced statistically significant higher pregnancy rates than the control group. It is important to find an outlet for conflicting emotions of grief, guilt, anger and regret, but also to recognise that these emotions are not unique to you, many couples who find themselves childless need to find the positive aspects of their lives.

There are also online support groups, Infertility Network and Fertility Friends provide excellent resource material and links with other similar sites.

Remember that good nutrition actually feeds the emotional body as well as the physical. For those couples who feel locked in a prison of anxiety and who have become overwhelmed by their inability to reproduce, the addition of the right amino acids may be the key to unlocking their fertility potential. Amino acids are potent supplements and should only be taken under the guidance of an experienced practitioner (see help list).

Alternative and complementary therapies

The most important first principles towards fertility are:

- Establish your nutritional status with a hair mineral analysis (see help list).
- Change to a wholefood organic diet (see chapter 3).
- Eliminate environmental toxins (see chapter 4).
- Eliminate any hidden infections (see chapter 4).
- Book a full osteopathic examination.

Osteopathic examination

This may seem a strange examination to undertake, particularly if you have no aches or pains. Checking the alignment of spine and pelvis has often uncovered small anomalies to which the body has adjusted and accommodated with very little in the way of pain or discomfort. A long-forgotten injury from childhood, for example, a fall from a horse or climbing frame, may have caused a slight displacement in the vertebral column. The spinal cord, which is the source of all nerve function, travels down the centre of the spine with branches of nerves spreading out between the spaces in the spinal column.

- Bodily functions are dependent upon their nerve supply – any slight interruption, likened to a flickering light bulb, compromises the organ the nerve is supplying. This could be any of the pelvic organs, including those essential to baby-making, ovaries, fallopian tubes or uterus in the woman, or the prostate gland and seminal tubes in the man.

- Women who have often lifted or carried weights, are more prone to pelvic displacement.

- The osteopathic mantra is 'function follows structure'.

Acupuncture

There are different types of acupuncture, which is an element of Chinese medicine, but fundamentally what acupuncture is attempting to achieve is balance and body harmony. The acupuncturist uses very fine needles inserted into various energy points under the skin. It is believed that the needling activates deep sensory nerves, which cause the pituitary to release chemicals known as endorphins. Endorphins are the body's own natural pain relievers and give us a feeling of wellbeing and harmony.

Deciding where to insert the needles is helped by feeling the pulse, not just for speed, but for depth and quality. Also, examination of the tongue will indicate where an imbalance lies.

'Five element' acupuncture has been found to be the most helpful for assisting fertility. The five elements are related to the five major organs of the body, those are the heart, lungs, liver, kidneys and spleen. All our organs work in harmony with each other and acupuncture attempts to restore the working harmony between these organs.

Research has shown that acupuncture performed 25 minutes before and after IVF embryo transfer increased pregnancy rates.

Always try to seek out an acupuncturist who is experienced in treating infertility. Please see the help list for further information.

Shiatsu

For those with an inbuilt fear of needles, shiatsu may be a valuable alternative. Originally from Japan, but based on similar principles to acupuncture, it aims to heal body, mind and spirit by balancing the flow of energy. The practitioner uses his fingertips, knuckles, elbows and sometimes feet, to give a relaxing and invigorating massage (see help list for more information).

Tai Chi

Tai Chi has been found to be very useful in controlling stress with a combination of 19 different movements and one pose. The technique originated from China where it was believed that certain movements combined with meditation help to restore energy.

Flower essences

There is no evidence to support the use of flower essences other than anecdotal accounts from users. However, flower essences are inexpensive and can be used safely and, from my own experience, couples like them. Their use certainly has a positive emotional effect.

Over many years flower and plant essences have been used to restore body harmony. There are many to choose from, however, I can recommend Australian Bush Flower Essences. The seed from She Oak is the same size

'"Five element" acupuncture has been found to be the most helpful for assisting fertility.'

as the human ovary and the flower looks like a fallopian tube. She Oak is used to regulate hormonal balance and can be taken safely with any orthodox medication. It is said to benefit those women who, for no apparent physical reason, are unable to become pregnant, by removing emotional blocks which interfere with conception.

She Oak dosage for infertility:

- Seven drops under the tongue night and morning.
- Take She Oak for one month and then a two week break.
- In the two week break take the essence Turkey Bush, for creativity.
- Continue this regime for six months.

Flannel Flower for low sperm count

Flannel Flower looks like the edelweiss which is a strong and hardy alpine flower, just the qualities we are looking for in sperm. Use the same regime as for She Oak.

Siberian ginseng

There is some truth to the advice 'take Siberian ginseng if you wish to become pregnant'. Ginseng has been used for centuries in folk medicine, particularly for male impotency. Research has shown that ginseng can improve sexual interest and performance. If you are taking medication, check with your GP before taking ginseng. Other herbs are also supportive of fertility, rhodiola, like ginseng, is an adaptogen allowing the body to maintain balance and harmony despite the stresses and strains of modern living. Both herbs improve circulation and energy while reducing irritability and anxiety. Pinus sibirica, is an oil extracted from the Siberian cedar and is said to improve sexual vitality in men.

Vitamin supplementation

It is always better to take specific nutrients according to your own test results (see chapter 8). Amino acids, particularly L-arginine is required for normal functioning of the pituitary gland and is essential for sexual health. The maximum dose of arginine for the treatment of low sperm count is 8g a day. It cannot be taken in isolation as, like many amino acids, arginine requires what we term as co-factors for absorption, these include vitamins C, B6, B1 and B2.

Summing Up

- Painful intercourse must be investigated in order to improve your chances of a pregnancy.

- A loss of interest in sex could be due to extreme stress and tiredness, or sometimes a side effect of prescribed medication.

- Group therapy should not be discounted as an option, it may be easier to talk to other people in the same situation and provide an outlet for difficult emotions.

- Alternative and complementary therapies can be useful when dealing with infertility. Osteopathy can find spine and pelvic misalignments which may be compromising fertility.

- Shiatsu and Tai Chi help unlock emotional blocks and are very relaxing techniques.

Chapter Nine

Assisted Reproductive Technologies

Once you have completed all the suggested natural pathways to good health and fertility and pregnancy remains elusive, then it may be time to seek out further medical treatment. Many career women put off pregnancy until they are in their 30s and think IVF (in vitro fertilisation) will always be there to provide a solution if nothing happens. It is more important to have regular sex, be patient, prepare your body for pregnancy and not rush down the IVF path too quickly.

Medical investigations have been discussed in previous chapters and it may be that assisted conception is the only way forward. It remains very important that you follow the guidelines for good health to give your body the best possible chance of conceiving with a successful outcome. Many failed attempts could be avoided by first preparing your body for conception. Remember, healthy eggs and healthy sperm require a highly nutritious diet.

On the 25th July 1978, Louise Brown, the world's first 'test tube' baby, was born. The history of assisted birth over the following 30 years has been revolutionary and today there are some 37,000 women undergoing IVF treatment in Britain. Less than one third of IVF cycles in women under the age of 35 are successful, figures from the British Fertility Society suggest about 14,000 births each year are as a result of IVF treatment. Infertility treatment only became available as a commercial operation in the 1990s and, although strictly regulated by the Human Fertilisation and Embryology Department, has allowed further developments of the original IVF treatment.

'On the 25th July 1978, Louise Brown, the world's first "test tube" baby, was born. The history of assisted birth over the following 30 years has been revolutionary and today there are some 37,000 women undergoing IVF treatment in Britain.'

At present in the UK, the National Institute for Clinical Excellence (NICE) recommend three cycles of IVF treatment for women aged between 23 and 39, providing they meet certain medical criteria. Sadly, not all health trusts accept this guidance and choose to ignore the recommendations. This is not surprising when cash-strapped trusts are continually looking to cut costs and IVF is not seen as a medical emergency.

The hospital trusts that do offer three cycles often put in place very restrictive conditions which make it impossible for a number of women. Those who already have one child, even from a previous relationship are not considered, those who smoke and those who are considered overweight will often be denied treatment even though this is contrary to NICE guidelines

Therefore, it is not surprising that couples often opt for private treatment. Of the 45,000 cycles performed each year in the UK, 75% of these are conducted privately.

Some private clinics will offer either free or reduced treatment in exchange for egg donation. This arrangement will only be available to those women who have a sufficient supply of eggs. The overwhelming desire for a child will see couples doing anything to achieve their goal. This inevitably creates a vulnerability which is in danger of being exploited by purely profit-centred clinics. There is also an increase in infertility tourism, where desperate couples seek help from less well-regulated clinics overseas.

IVF

In vitro simply means 'in glass'. Prior to 1978, fertilisation was by the natural route, i.e. sperm meets egg inside the woman's body, but IVF offered fertilisation in a glass test tube. The resulting embryo is then transferred into the uterus, where it is hoped it will develop into a foetus and then a baby. This procedure has brought tremendous joy to many couples, but also huge disappointment for those couples when the procedure does not work. Stress levels can become out of control and expert counselling is advised before embarking upon this route. It is far better to know what to expect and to be prepared for failure.

Availability of IVF treatment varies from region to region and country to country. Although treatment is available on the NHS, this is limited and many couples end up funding the treatment themselves, which is often an added anxiety, particularly for those couples who experience failed attempts.

There are numerous private clinics offering IVF treatment. When choosing the clinic, always ask for their success rate and their failure rate. You also need to be assured of the experience and competence of the doctor treating you. Ask to see your practitioner's CV and ask how long they have been doing this work. Compare costs and be prepared to travel to get the best possible service. The service provided by a clinic is variable so it's important to check that the clinic is the right one for you.

Each attempt at IVF is called a 'cycle' and begins by suppression of the natural menstrual cycle. Drugs are administered by a nasal spray which inhibit the production of FSH. The next stage is to stimulate the ovaries to develop several Graafian follicles to ensure eggs will reach maturity. Synthetic hormones are taken either orally or by injection and ultrasound scans and blood tests will monitor progress. Measurements are also taken of the womb lining as this must be ready to receive the embryo.

Depending upon the results of blood tests, the amount of synthetic hormones will be increased or reduced accordingly. You may be asked to inject yourself with the synthetic hormones.

Egg retrieval

Egg retrieval can be an anxious time as many couples believe the more eggs that are collected, the better their chances are of fertilisation. However, it is egg quality that is most important. Retrieval is performed with a light sedation and does not usually take longer than half an hour. A vaginal ultrasound probe is used and eggs are removed from the follicles using a long syringe called an aspirating needle. The syringe sucks out the fluid from the follicle containing the eggs, between five and 10 eggs are removed in a typical retrieval, although this is dependent upon how many follicles have reached maturity.

The eggs are then viewed under a microscope and graded to determine which eggs retrieved are suitable for fertilisation. At the same time your partner will be asked to produce semen from masturbation into a sterile container, this can be

'When choosing the clinic, always ask for their success rate and their failure rate. You also need to be assured of the experience and competence of the doctor treating you. Ask to see your practitioner's CV and ask how long they have been doing this work.'

a little embarrassing for some people and care must be taken to ensure this is done with privacy and confidence. The semen is then washed and spun in a special machine, called a centrifuge, to extract the sperms. Only the strongest survive this process.

The eggs and sperms are then mixed together in a glass dish and left overnight in an incubator which maintains the dish at normal body temperature. The following morning the dish will be examined under a microscope to see if any embryos are developing, and after 48 hours embryos will be ready for transfer to your uterus. As there are numerous complications associated with multiple births, only one or two embryos are transferred, in the hope that at least one of them will implant and develop naturally to become a foetus and eventually a healthy baby.

Any unused embryos will be frozen and used for further attempts at a later date. This is a major advance as it reduces the need for further interventions to retrieve more eggs. There are strict rules concerning embryo storage. After five years you will be consulted to discuss either their use or disposal.

Two weeks after transfer, a standard pregnancy test will reveal if IVF has been successful.

Blastocyst transfer

A blastocyst transfer simply means leaving the developing embryo longer than 48 hours in the glass dish prior to transfer into the uterus. A blastocyst is a highly developed embryo which has divided many times and in theory has a better chance of implantation. Only one blastocyst is transferred so there is no risk of a multiple pregnancy. Blastocyst transfer is often more acceptable to older women, between the ages of 38 and 44, who have a number of embryos but a lower chance of pregnancy because of their age. Blastocyst selection can offer the best possible chance of implantation.

'Blastocyst transfer is often more acceptable to older women, between the ages of 38 and 44, who have a number of embryos but a lower chance of pregnancy because of their age.'

Variations of IVF

Natural cycle IVF

Natural cycle IVF can only be used if you have a regular cycle. This is thought to be a slightly safer procedure as no fertility drugs are used, however only one egg will be retrieved which occurs with a natural cycle.

Intracytoplasmic sperm injection (ICSI)

This is often the chosen route for couples where the male partner has either a very low sperm count or the sperm are held back in the testes. Recovery of sperm is possible from a fine needle inserted into the scrotum.

In the process of ICSI an individual sperm is injected directly into the egg. This technique bypasses the normal competition where only the healthiest sperm reach the egg for fertilisation.

Since the introduction of legislation requiring sperm donors to agree to be identified to their offspring in adulthood, there has been a dramatic reduction in sperm donation. For some couples, having their own genetically identified baby is all important, however the quality of the sperm and egg should always be a priority.

Sub-zonal insemination (SUZI)

SUZI is where several sperms are injected just inside the membrane of the egg. This method increases the chance of fertilisation and is used particularly where the male partner has a persistently low sperm count.

IVF using donor eggs, sperms or embryos

Sperm donation has been used for many years if the male partner is infertile. There was always a constant supply of sperm donors, often medical students who were paid a nominal amount for this service. In recent years, donation has come under legal scrutiny and the anonymity of the donor is no longer allowed. This has caused a drop in willing donors as men are reluctant to face any resulting children who would have a legal right to contact them at a later date. The legislation was established to enable offspring to trace their birth father and for some, to reduce emotional anxieties over genetic inheritance.

Egg donation, or egg sharing, is less common but an essential service to a woman who is unable to produce her own eggs even when her ovaries are stimulated.

Embryo donation may be considered if one or both partners are infertile or there is a serious risk of passing on an inherited disease.

Gamete intrafallopian transfer (GIFT)

Rather than transfer a two-day old embryo, as in IVF, eggs are removed from the ovaries and the healthiest are selected and placed together with sperm in the fallopian tubes. Fertilisation therefore takes place in the body, as it would if conception occurred naturally.

In vitro maturation (IVM)

In IVM the eggs are removed from the ovaries and are collected when they are still immature. They are then matured in the laboratory before being fertilised. This has the advantage that the woman does not need to take large doses of hormonal drugs before the eggs can be collected as with conventional IVF, when mature eggs are collected.

Donor insemination

After careful monitoring of the woman's natural cycle, donor sperm is placed high in the vagina or uterus at the time of ovulation. Artificial insemination can be from either a regular partner or a donor.

Donor sperm is screened for sexually transmitted diseases and for some genetic disorders before use.

Rise of IVF

▒ Some 37,000 patients undergo IVF treatments in Britain each year.

▒ About 14,000, or 1.8%, of babies each year are born through IVF.

▒ About 14% of couples have difficulty conceiving.

▒ Less than a third, 32%, of IVF cycles in women under the age of 35 are successful.

▒ The average cost of an IVF cycle is £5,000.

Source: Human Fertilisation and Embryology Authority, NHS.

Surrogacy

Surrogacy is when another woman carries and gives birth to a baby for you. The pregnancy may be initiated by use of your own eggs, donor eggs or the surrogate's own eggs. It may be via sperm from your partner or donor sperm. There are various permutations, but what is essential is a legal framework to be established prior to embarking upon this route.

Points to consider include:

▒ It is illegal to advertise that you are looking for a surrogate or willing to be one.

▒ Commercial 'rent a womb' is illegal. Only reasonable expenses can be paid to the surrogate.

▒ Surrogacy agreements are unenforceable in UK courts of law.

▒ A surrogate mother, under UK law, is the legal mother and has up to six weeks to change her mind about the agreement.

▒ A parental order must be sought to confer full parental status on both the intended parents.

Explaining surrogacy to children can be a sensitive issue and this should be considered before embarking upon any style of assisted pregnancy.

'About 14,000 or 1.8% of babies each year are born through IVF.'

Human Fertilisation and Embryology Authority, NHS.

Honesty is usually the best option and if you are open with your child about the way in which they were conceived, it should minimise awkward situations later in their lives.

Side effects

Fertility treatments, like all medical treatments, are not immune from risk. Discuss the possible side effects in detail with your healthcare professional before you decide on treatment. Many clinics now provide a counselling service which is worth asking about, finding an understanding ear can prevent emotions spilling over and affecting your ability to manage work or relationships both with your partner, family and friends.

'Fertility treatments, like all medical treatments, are not immune from risk. Discuss the possible side effects in detail with your healthcare professional before you decide on treatment.'

Fertility drugs

Gonadotropins are the hormonal fertility drugs given either by nasal spray, by mouth or by injection. They contain FSH, LH, and sometimes human chorionic gonadotropin (Hcg), which is similar to LH and stimulates the natural LH surge, that causes ovulation.

Gonadotropins are used to induce follicle development and ovulation in women who do not ovulate. They are also used to induce development and ovulation of multiple follicles in women undergoing assisted fertilisation. Careful monitoring of patients is essential to reduce the potential for side effects, which may include:

- Ovarian hyperstimulation syndrome – characterised by enlarged ovaries and fluid collecting in the abdomen after ovulation or egg retrieval. The mild form occurs in 10-20% of cycles and although uncomfortable, symptoms quickly resolve. In the severe form, which occurs in about 1% of all cases, hospitalisation is necessary where with regular monitoring of blood oestrogen, symptoms are brought under control.

- Multiple babies – there is a risk that the hormonal drugs, particularly clomifene will produce too many eggs. Without the use of fertility medication, there is a natural 1-2% chance of producing two or more babies naturally; after taking a fertility medication, that chance increases to

30%. Compared to a single baby, twins, triplets, quads or more, pose an increased risk of pregnancy loss, premature delivery, infant abnormalities, handicap due to a very premature birth, and increased risk to the mother of high blood pressure, haemorrhage and other significant maternal complications. The natural exuberance from parents at finally having a pregnancy must be tempered with knowledge of these increased risks to both mother and child. As mentioned in earlier chapters, counselling is particularly important prior to embarking upon any form of assisted fertility treatment.

- Ovarian twisting – this is a very rare side effect occurring only occasionally in less than 1% of gonadotropin cycles, the stimulated ovary can twist on itself, cutting off blood supply. Surgery is then required to remove the ovary.

- Emotional stress – couples describe infertility treatment as a waiting game and an emotional roller coaster, one minute feeling hugely optimistic then negative results bringing despair. Frustration, irritability, anger and guilt are some of the emotions you can expect to experience. Very few couples avoid tearful confrontations so you may want to find an understanding counsellor prior to treatment. It can be much easier to talk with someone you have already met and have developed a relationship with.

- Ectopic pregnancy – an ectopic pregnancy occurs when an embryo decides to implant outside the uterus. Fallopian tubes are particularly vulnerable and can rupture under the pressure, this causes internal bleeding and is an emergency situation. The tube is irreparably damaged which further complicates infertility. The chances of an ectopic pregnancy are higher in women receiving IVF. In most cases the cause is unknown, but research has indicated that 11 in 1,000 IVF pregnancies will end in an ectopic. (Tay et al, 2000; Seeber & Bonhart 2008)

Other reported side effects include:

- Bloating and fluid retention with ankle swelling.

- Breast tenderness, which for some women is particularly uncomfortable.

- Tiredness, exhaustion and a complete lack of energy.

- Digestive upsets and a feeling of nausea.

Finding a clinic

The most important first step when looking for a clinic is to ensure it is registered with HFEA. Their registration certificate should be displayed in a prominent position, if not, ask to see it.

First impressions count. You should find a relaxed and friendly atmosphere where the staff are supportive and encouraging. This is very important as you will be making frequent visits to the clinic.

Location

This may seem totally irrelevant, but frequent visits to a clinic miles away from your home is an added inconvenience. Travelling can be costly, time-consuming and frustrating. Try to find a clinic which is close to your home. You may be able to have certain tests at your local hospital and travel to your chosen clinic for treatment, although you may find your local NHS trust are not open to working in this way.

Staff

Do not be afraid to ask about the experience of all the staff, including the doctors, nurses and laboratory technicians. Find out how many years they have been doing this work and what their qualifications are.

Success rates

Directly comparing success rates of clinics is not very helpful as clinics often differ in the type of conditions they are treating. Some clinics have an age barrier and do not treat patients with complicated diagnoses so inevitably their results may appear superior.

HFEA produce an online 'Choose a Fertility Clinic' guide (www.hfea.gov.uk/fertility-clinic-guide.html) with data on every licensed clinic showing the number of treatments, the number of pregnancies and the number of live births each year. The guide will show a clinic's success rate in three ways:

'The most important first step when looking for a clinic is to ensure it is registered with HFEA. Their registration certificate should be displayed in a prominent position, if not, ask to see it.'

- Success rates compared with the national average.

- The number of treatment cycles performed and how many of those cycles resulted in a live birth.

- The predicted chance of a woman having a live birth if treated at this clinic.

Services offered

Find out if this clinic can offer the treatment you are looking for. Other questions you should ask when contacting them include:

- Do they provide counselling or any other supportive help?

- Do they have a cancellation policy?

- How many treatments are offered before a different approach is discussed?

- What is their embryo transfer policy? Clinics can replace up to two embryos at each attempt at IVF or up to three if you are aged 40 or over and using your own eggs. Single embryo transfer offers the least risk of a complicated pregnancy.

Your first visit to the clinic

Be prepared. Make a list of questions beforehand, write them down and do not feel embarrassed to ask for all the information you require to make an informed decision. Remember you are planning your baby's birthday and the decisions you make today are important not just to fulfil your own desire, but to ensure the future health of your unborn baby.

The doctor must make an assessment of your general health prior to any decision about ART. HFEA also require the clinic to carry out a 'welfare of the child assessment' before starting any treatment. This will involve a detailed questionnaire to allow the physician to make a judgement as to whether the treatment is likely to cause serious physical, psychological or medical harm to any children born or to any existing children of the family. They also take into account any existing factors which may cause serious physical, psychological or medical harm to any child born or to any existing children of the family.

Consent to treatment

Consent forms are a legal requirement and you must fully understand what your treatment involves, what the potential side effects are and importantly, that there are no guarantees of success. Once you have had time to investigate these matters and reflect upon all possible outcomes, then you are at liberty to sign the consent form.

There are four different types of consent:

- Consent for ART. This is just like any other medical consent form, although you must consent to both egg retrieval and the transfer of embryos into your uterus.

- Consent is required for using your eggs, sperm or embryos for your own treatment, for the treatment of others and for research purposes. You also need to consent to the storage of your eggs, sperm and embryos for a defined period of time before they are destroyed.

- The clinic cannot give any information regarding your treatment to your GP, counsellor or family member without your permission. Consent to the release of this information must be considered carefully.

- Consent to parenthood. It may be necessary if you are using either donated eggs or sperm, that you or your partner consent to be the legal parent of the child.

Finance

Financial pressure is what often drives would-be parents apart. In their desperation to have a family they lose their normal sense of budget control. It is like being on a never-ending treadmill where you have lost the ability to 'get off'. Knowing when to make the decision to stop treatment is extremely difficult. I have known couples remortgage their home, borrow from their parents and still run up debts which take years to repay. Starting a family with no money will bring additional strains on even the most secure of partnerships.

Infertility treatment is available on the NHS at no direct financial cost. However, as previously stated, Health Trusts often have their own criteria on who they will accept for treatment. You will need a referral letter from your GP as a starting point. NHS funding can cover the cost of IVF and ICSI.

Remember that fertility drugs will be subject to the usual prescription charges (unless you hold an exemption certificate) and these can become very costly. Ask your consultant to approximate how many prescriptions you will require during the course of treatment so you have a better idea of cost before you embark on a treatment cycle.

Due to the limited availability of NHS treatment, it is not surprising that many couples opt for private clinics. Prices can vary and it is important that you get a full breakdown of all costs prior to starting treatment. Clinics are regulated by HFEA, although they do not regulate fees.

- The certification and inspection costs incurred by HFEA may be passed on to you, not all clinics do this, but be aware this may be an extra charge, usually about £100. However, as clinics are competing for clients, prices are usually in a similar range.

- Some clinics offer a free initial consultation, while others charge between £100 and £200 for this.

- Each visit will incur a consultation cost of between £100 and £200

Assisted techniques

An average cost for IVF would be £3,000 to £5,000. Additional procedures, including ICSI, will incur a further average cost of £1,000. Prices will increase considerably when using either donor sperm or donor eggs.

- One cycle, which will include egg collection and preparation – £2,000 to £3,000.

- Semen assessment tests – £100 to £200.

- Blood tests – £100 to £200.

- Anaesthetic fees are usually not included in the overall fee, and work as an extra £200 to £300 charge.

- Drugs can be particularly expensive and it may be worth budgeting for £500 as an additional cost.
- Ultrasound scans – £160 per scan.
- Embryo freezing – £2,000 to £3,000.
- Embryo storage – £300 per annum.
- Sperm storage – £300 per annum.
- Frozen embryo transfer – £1,000.

IVF costs of one cycle, plus semen tests and blood tests, drugs and anaesthetic costs cannot be avoided. However, you may be able to negotiate on ultrasound scans and storage costs.

Summing Up

▦ Prepare your body for ART and speak with your healthcare professional about the best course of treatment for you and your partner. Be patient, treatment does take time.

▦ The side effects from fertility drugs can be very debilitating, you should speak with your healthcare professional about the risks and if possible, make an appointment with a counsellor before embarking upon treatment so you are familiar and comfortable with them.

▦ Find a clinic that is in a convenient location, registered with HFEA and that has experienced staff. Use HFEA's website facility to find and research suitable clinics.

▦ Make sure you know how much your treatment is likely to cost and budget in for any unforeseen costs that might come up.

▦ Discuss the financial pressure with your partner and make a decision together about how you will cope with the financial strain.

Chapter Ten

So You Think You are Pregnant

At the end of the first cycle you are anxiously waiting for a period that does not appear, emotions will be running very high, am I pregnant or is this is a false alarm?

There are a number of shop-bought pregnancy testing kits available. The test is designed to measure the amount of beta human chorionic gonadotropin (hCG) in the urine. HCG is produced approximately seven days after fertilisation, but takes a further seven days to appear in the urine. Do wait until you have missed a period for a more accurate result. These tests are reasonably accurate if you carefully follow the instructions in the box. Early morning testing is advised as the level of hCG accumulates overnight. Occasionally a false negative occurs, so keep calm and test again after two days if your period has not started.

If you are under the care of a fertility specialist, then the clinic you are attending will want to confirm the diagnosis with an early morning specimen of your urine. You may also be offered a blood test which can confirm the presence of hCG before your period is due. Remember there is a cost for this blood test unless it has been included in your overall package of ART. Each individual fertility clinic will have their own policy governing this issue. The blood test will confirm fertilisation has taken place, but may also show that implantation has not yet occurred. In these circumstances, a repeat blood test after a few days will be recommended.

Emotional issues

Once your pregnancy has been confirmed, your initial joy may be overshadowed by the anxieties that all new would-be parents face. Concerns that the pregnancy will continue to full term and concerns that the baby will be well.

For parents who have undergone ART, these concerns are magnified and many do not feel the elation they expected. The initial joy and intense relief is quickly replaced by anxieties whether the pregnancy will be normal. Feelings of fear and nervousness are normal.

Try to stay positive, although I know you will be acutely aware of any small change in your body, every ache and every normal symptom will signal catastrophe. It is not unusual for pregnancies conceived by IVF, to display some minor 'spotting' (fresh blood visible from the vagina). This does not necessarily signal disaster, however you should speak with your consultant if you experience this. Statistically, miscarriage is more common in the first trimester (first three months of pregnancy) this applies to all women however they conceived. If you have miscarried before, this is a particularly anxious time and you are unlikely to relax until you have passed the point of where your previous pregnancy or pregnancies came to grief. Once you have the results of an ultrasound scan and you can see your developing baby, confidence will be restored.

Where to give birth

Fertility specialists are not necessarily active obstetricians, so the decision of what to do next should have been considered prior to conception. Some couples who have opted for private fertility treatment, now decide to return to the NHS system for antenatal care and delivery. Some private clinics work with certain obstetricians on a private basis and see the pregnancy through to full term and delivery. The choice is yours, and which road you now take may be determined by cost alone.

The best advice is to see your GP as soon as possible and discuss your options with him or her. Your GP will know what is available in your area. Many areas operate what is called a 'shared care' system, between your GP, midwife and hospital consultant.

What is important is that you book into a system of care, whether hospital or home, as soon as you know you are pregnant. All pregnancies are special, but if you have endured years of infertility, then your pregnancy is a little extra special and all possible care will be open to you. You may be classed as a 'high risk pregnancy' if you are an older woman or have received ART. This is not to say that the pregnancy will be abnormal, just really a medical classification to ensure you receive the best possible care.

When do we tell family and friends?

Once a pregnancy is confirmed, the decision of when to share your joy with family and friends can also present a challenge. An immediate response may be to shout from the hilltops or the reverse, to keep absolutely silent until the pregnancy is well established and you feel sufficiently confident that the pregnancy will survive.

Many couples choose to tell only very close family or friends until the end of the first three months. Again, the choice is yours and the best advice is to follow your own instinct on this issue.

Advice for early pregnancy

Pregnancy causes some huge physiological changes in your body and although these changes are normal, you will feel tired. The tiredness can be completely overwhelming. Rest as much as you can in the first three months until the pregnancy is well established. We are all used to hectic schedules, but slow down and put your feet up as much as possible.

During the first trimester the desire for sex often diminishes, women feel tired and sometimes nauseated. However, in the second trimester (three to six months) sexual desire may heighten as increased blood supply to the genitals makes orgasm more easily achieved.

'You may be classed as a "high risk pregnancy" if you are an older woman or have received ART. This is not to say that the pregnancy will be abnormal, just really a medical classification to ensure you receive the best possible care.'

In the last trimester (six to nine months), the increasing weight of the tummy may make sex awkward and difficult to achieve. Experimenting with different positions is the key!

Avoid strenuous sexual activity in the first three months and refrain altogether for a few weeks if there has been any bleeding or spotting.

Also, keep to your healthy diet and avoid alcohol completely.

Early signs and symptoms of pregnancy:

- Tender swollen breasts, sensitive to touch.
- Frequency of passing urine.
- Overwhelming feeling of tiredness.
- Feeling very sick.
- Overly emotional.

For more information see *Your First Pregnancy – An Essential Guide* or *Pregnancy: Older Women – The Essential Guide* (Need2Know).

What happens when nothing happens?

If you have had several unsuccessful attempts at assisted conception, it may be time to take a break, and reflect on your priorities and the important things in your life. Accepting a life without children takes time and adjustment, giving up the prospect of your own children is like bereavement.

Try to make a decision that will satisfy both you and your life partner. If you are unable to do this, seek out an experienced counsellor and discuss the situation with your chosen consultant. Being parents together may have been your goal, but grieving for what might have been is self-destructive.

When you have made your decision, stick to it. Celebrate the life you have and the freedom from visits to the clinic, raised hopes and deflated dreams, the future lies ahead with new experiences and challenges.

'Accepting a life without children takes time and adjustment, giving up the prospect of your own children is like bereavement.'

During the long and difficult journey to achieve a baby by assisted conception, the overriding pressure is to have your own genetic child or one with at least the DNA from one partner, rarely is any discussion given to adoption. Couples may resent the intrusiveness of the adoption process after spending years going through infertility treatments.

However, families today are often made up of step children due to divorce and remarriage, so the whole issue of genetics or having your own biological child becomes less important. Families are made, not born. Adoption can produce a much wanted child where the family bond between parent and child is equally as strong and as rewarding. Maybe giving a child a chance to live a loving life will be more satisfying than making a life. For more information on adoption, see *Adoption and Fostering – The Essential Guide* (Need2Know).

'Families are made, not born. Adoption can produce a much wanted child where the family bond between parent and child is equally as strong and as rewarding.'

Summing Up

- Infertility is a challenge and one best faced together. It is my hope that this book has given you a deeper insight into the causes of your infertility and what you can both do to improve your fertility chances. Do not let infertility be the cause of serious rift in your relationship.

- Once you embark upon ART, keep your faith with each other, and remember to talk together. From experience, women often want to discuss every minute detail but men prefer to leave talking to the doctor and shy away from in-depth discussion. Remember to honour each other's needs.

- It is my sincere wish that you are successful in your attempts at baby-making and I wish your future baby the happiest of birthdays.

Help List

British Acupuncture Council

63 Jeddo Road, London, W12 9HQ
Tel: 020 8735 0400
www.acupuncture.org.uk
A website with lots of information about acupuncture and how to find a practitioner near you.

British Association of Nutritional Therapists (BANT)

27 Old Gloucester Street, London, WC1N 3XX
Tel: 0870 6061284
www.bant.org.uk
Information on where to find a nutritionist near you can be found on BANT's website.

British Infertility Counselling Association (BICA)

www.bica.net
BICA try to ensure the highest standards of counselling and support offered to couples experiencing fertility issues. Their website has a 'find a counsellor' facility.

Daisy Network

PO Box 392, High Wycombe, Bucks, HP15 7SH
www.daisynetwork.org.uk
The Daisy Network provides support for women who have experienced premature menopause.

Dr Michel Odent

michelodent@googlemail.com
www.wombecology.com
Information on the 'Accordion Method' of pre-conceptual care.

Fertility Education Trust

www.fertilityet.org.uk
Information on fertility awareness and free downloadable temperature charts.

Fertility Friends

www.fertilityfriends.co.uk
A large online community of people experiencing infertility issues, providing support and information on treatments, success rates, further reading, parenting and adoption.

Foresight

178 Hawthorn Road, West Bognor, West Sussex, PO21 2UY
Tel: 01243 868001
foresighthq@btopenworld.com
www.foresight-preconception.org.uk
Foresight is a registered charity providing pre-conceptual care, including mineral hair analysis. Foresight also provides information, supplements and various publications.

Geneva Diagnostics

356 West Barnes Lane, New Malden, Surrey, PO21 2UY
Tel: 0208 336 7750
www.gdx.uk.net
For access to mineral hair analysis, stool and blood tests.

Infertility Network

www.infertilitynetworkuk.com
An online infertility support network.

Marilyn Glenville PhD

www.marilynglenville.com
Marilyn Glenville is a nutritional specialist with an interest in fertility. The website has an online shop where you can purchase supplements recommended by Marilyn for a range of conditions.

Miscarriage Association

C/O Clayton Hospital, Northgate, Wakefield, West Yorkshire, WF1 3JS
Tel: 0131 334 8883 (helpline)
info@miscarriageassociation.org.uk
www.miscarriageassociation.org.uk
Provides support and information for people suffering the effects of pregnancy loss.

National Endometriosis Society

50 Westminster Palace Gardens, Artillery Row, London, SW1P 1RL
Tel: 0808 808 2227 (helpline)
www.endo.org.uk
Provides support and information to women living with endometriosis.

National Institute of Medical Herbalists

www.nimh.org.uk
Information about medical herbalists and a search facility to find a practitioner in your area.

Naturopathic Association

www.naturopathy.org.uk
The Naturopathic Association hold a register of naturopaths who will help with diet issues.

Surrogacy Network

www.surrogacyuk.org
Offers support and information to those interested in surrogacy in the UK.

The Human Fertilisation and Embryology Authority (HFEA)

Paxton House, 30 Artillery Lane, London, E1 7LS
Tel: 020 7377 5077
www.hfea.gov.uk
Lots of information about infertility and treatments, they also have a 'find a clinic' facility.

Verity

The Grayston Centre, 28 Charles Square, London, N1 6HT
www.verity-pcos.org.uk
Verity is a registered charity to support sufferers of polycystic ovary syndrome.

Yes Baby

www.yesyesyes.org
Fertility-friendly intimate products.

Glossary

Amino acids
The building blocks from which body protein is made.

Assisted reproductive technology (ART)
The collective name for medical infertility treatments.

Cervical mucus
Secretions into the vagina from the cervix.

Cervix
The narrow neck of the uterus which protrudes into the vagina.

Embryo
A fertilised egg which has the ability to develop into a foetus.

Fertilisation

Penetration of an egg by a sperm producing an embryo. Natural fertilisation takes place in a woman's body but it can also occur in the laboratory (in vitro).

Foetus
The term given to an embryo after eight weeks of development up until birth.

Follicle-stimulating hormone (FSH)
A hormone released from the pituitary gland that stimulates follicle production. It is also used in ART to stimulate the production of several follicles.

Gonadotropins
Sex hormones released by the pituitary gland to produce sperm and mature eggs.

Graafian follicle
A small mature sac in the ovary in which the egg develops.

Human chorionic gonadotropin (hCG)
A hormone produced to maintain a pregnancy and is excreted in the urine indicating a pregnancy. This is how a pregnancy test detects its result.

Hormones
Chemical messengers which co-ordinate body and mind function.

HFEA
Human Fertilisation and Embryology Authority.

Impotence
A man's inability to gain an erection.

Insemination
The artificial planting of sperm into a female reproductive tract.

Luteinising hormone (LH)
Hormone released by the pituitary gland, essential for the development of eggs and sperm.

Menstrual cycle
A woman's monthly cycle where an egg is released from the ovary, the lining of the uterus develops and sheds in the menstrual period, unless a pregnancy develops.

Ovarian hyperstimulation syndrome
A serious complication following drug-induced ovulation.

Ovary
The female reproduction organ that contains and releases eggs.

Ph
A measure of the hydrogen ions in a solution which produce either acidity or alkalinity.

Phytates
Any poisonous substance (toxin) produced by a plant.

Pituitary gland
The master endocrine gland.

Polycystic ovaries
The ovaries increase in size and develop cysts.

Premature menopause
Ovarian failure before the age of 40-45.

Spermatid
An immature sperm cell.

Trans fat
Produced when a particular form of hydrogen is bubbled through a vegetable fat.

Uterus
The womb where the embryo develops.

Need - 2 - Know

Available Titles Include ...

Allergies A Parent's Guide
ISBN 978-1-86144-064-8 £8.99

Autism A Parent's Guide
ISBN 978-1-86144-069-3 £8.99

Blood Pressure The Essential Guide
ISBN 978-1-86144-067-9 £8.99

Dyslexia and Other Learning Difficulties
A Parent's Guide ISBN 978-1-86144-042-6 £8.99

Bullying A Parent's Guide
ISBN 978-1-86144-044-0 £8.99

Epilepsy The Essential Guide
ISBN 978-1-86144-063-1 £8.99

Your First Pregnancy The Essential Guide
ISBN 978-1-86144-066-2 £8.99

Gap Years The Essential Guide
ISBN 978-1-86144-079-2 £8.99

Secondary School A Parent's Guide
ISBN 978-1-86144-093-8 £9.99

Primary School A Parent's Guide
ISBN 978-1-86144-088-4 £9.99

Applying to University The Essential Guide
ISBN 978-1-86144-052-5 £8.99

ADHD The Essential Guide
ISBN 978-1-86144-060-0 £8.99

Student Cookbook – Healthy Eating The Essential Guide
ISBN 978-1-86144-069-3 £8.99

Multiple Sclerosis The Essential Guide
ISBN 978-1-86144-086-0 £8.99

Coeliac Disease The Essential Guide
ISBN 978-1-86144-087-7 £9.99

Special Educational Needs A Parent's Guide
ISBN 978-1-86144-116-4 £9.99

The Pill An Essential Guide
ISBN 978-1-86144-058-7 £8.99

University A Survival Guide
ISBN 978-1-86144-072-3 £8.99

View the full range at **www.need2knowbooks.co.uk**. To order our titles call **01733 898103**, email **sales@ n2kbooks.com** or visit the website. Selected ebooks available online.

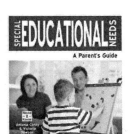

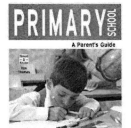

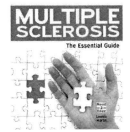

Need - 2 - Know, Remus House, Coltsfoot Drive, Peterborough, PE2 9BF